Kid's Box
New Generation

Caroline Nixon &
Michael Tomlinson

Workbook
with Digital Pack

6

American English

Thanks and Acknowledgments

Authors' thanks

Many thanks to everyone at Cambridge University Press & Assessment for their dedication and hard work, and in particular to:

Liane Grainger and Lynn Townsend for supervising the whole project and guiding us calmly through the storms. Alison Bewsher for her keen editorial eye, enthusiasm, and great suggestions.

Louise Wood for doing such a great job overseeing the level.

Liz Wilkie for her hard work and great editorial assistance.

We would also like to thank all our students and colleagues, past, present, and future, at Star English academy in Murcia, especially Jim Kelly for his friendship and support throughout the years.

Dedications

For Alison Sharpe for seeing the potential, for Maria Pylas for driving it forward, for Susan González for believing in and championing it, and for Liane Grainger for keeping us excellent, steadfast company throughout the whole of our stellar journey.

The authors and publishers acknowledge the following sources of copyright material and are grateful for the permissions granted. While every effort has been made, it has not always been possible to identify the sources of all the material used or to trace all copyright holders. If any omissions are brought to our notice; we will be happy to include the appropriate acknowledgments on reprinting and in the next update to the digital edition; as applicable.

Key: U = Unit, V= Values

Photography

The following photos are sourced from Getty Images.

U0: brunorbs/iStock/Getty Images Plus; C Squared Studios/Photodisc; pagadesign/E+; studiocasper/E+; goir/iStock/Getty Images Plus; Dynamic Graphics Group; Peter Dazeley/The Image Bank; alexey_boldin/iStock/Getty Images Plus; Wattanaphob Kappago/EyeEm; frender/iStock/Getty Images Plus; davidf/iStock/Getty Images Plus; domin_domin/iStock/Getty Images Plus; UmbertoPantalone/iStock/Getty Images Plus; vectorshape/iStock/Getty Images Plus; Inside Creative House/iStock/Getty Images Plus; Cavan Images; JohnnyGreig/iStock/Getty Images Plus; Phynart Studio/E+; SDI Productions/E+; 'Volodymyr Kryshtal/iStock/Getty Images Plus; Tatiana Pankova/iStock/Getty Images Plus, 'kolotuschenko/iStock/Getty Images Plu, Nik01ay/iStock/Getty Images Plus; Tatiana Pankova/iStock/Getty Images Plus; Polina Tomtosova/iStock/Getty Images Plus; Chris Daborn/iStock/Getty Images Plus; gmm2000/iStock/Getty Images Plus; Farbai/iStock/Getty Images Plus; Katrin Ray Shumakov/Moment; **U1:** Glowimages; Jose Luis Pelaez Inc/DigitalVision; Aleksandr Zubkov/Moment; Anna Erastova/iStock/Getty Images Plus, Sussenn/iStock/Getty Images Plus; **U2:** Marko Geber/DigitalVision; Jonathan Knowles/Stone; Sigrid Gombert/Image Source; Ramberg/E+; 3DSculptor/iStock/Getty Images Plus; Space Frontiers/Archive Photos; R_Type/iStock/Getty Images Plus; Tara Moore/DigitalVision; GlinskajaOlga/iStock/Getty Images Plus; Panuwat Sikham/iStock/Getty Images Plus; bennyb/iStock/Getty Images Plus; Anna Erastova/iStock/Getty Images Plus; PeterSnow/iStock/Getty Images Plus; **U3:** Capuski/E+; adamkaz/E+; Suriyapong Thongsawang/Moment; Caia Image/Collection Mix Subjects; FatCamera/E+; Ishii Koji/DigitalVision; lumpynoodles/DigitalVision Vectors; vectorsmarket/iStock/Getty Images Plus; Smashing Stocks/iStock/Getty Images Plus; JuliarStudio/iStock/Getty Images Plus; CasarsaGuru/E+; mgstudyo/iStock/Getty Images Plus; Arman Zhenikeyev/Corbis; Clive Brunskill/Getty Images Sport; Farbai/iStock/Getty Images Plus; vav63/iStock/Getty Images Plus; Alina Ermokhina/iStock/Getty Images Plus; Good_Stock/iStock/Getty Images Plus; seamartini/iStock/Getty Images Plus; LizaLutik/iStock/Getty Images Plus; Anna Erastova/iStock/Getty Images Plus; **U4:** R.Tsubin/Moment; EasyBuy4u/iStock/Getty Images Plus; Kuzmik_A/iStock/Getty Images Plus; Nattawut Lakjit/EyeEm; Burazin/The Image Bank; Yevgen Romanenko/Moment; Tomas_Mina/iStock/Getty Images Plus; HEX; Morsa Images/DigitalVision; Richard Bailey/Corbis Documentary; Ana Silva/EyeEm; Maskot; Jonathan Kirn/The Image Bank; yalcinsonat1/iStock/Getty Images Plus; Ruta Lipskija/EyeEm; jayvo86/iStock/Getty Images Plus; irem01/iStock/Getty Images Plus; Tetiana Garkusha/iStock/Getty Images Plus; Michael Burrell/iStock/Getty Images Plus; akiyoko/iStock/Getty Images Plus; Rawf8/iStock/Getty Images Plus; Blackholy/iStock/Getty Images Plus; SGAPhoto/iStock/Getty Images Plus; urfinguss/iStock/Getty Images Plus; Elva Etienne/Moment; fleaz/iStock/Getty Images Plus; neyro2008/iStock/Getty Images Plus; LizaLutik/iStock/Getty Images Plus; Aleksangel/iStock/Getty Images Plus; golubovy/iStock/Getty Images Plus; Anna Erastova/iStock/Getty Images Plus; PeterSnow/iStock/Getty Images Plus; **U5:** VivianG/iStock/Getty Images Plus; Humberto Ramirez/Moment; Reinhard Dirscherl/The Image Bank; Gabrielle Yap/EyeEm; Raimundo Fernandez Diez/Moment; Andrew Peacock/Stone; by wildestanimal/Moment; piola666/E+; Lunamarina/iStock/Getty Images Plus; David Madison/DigitalVision; Patrick J. Endres/Corbis Documentary; evemilla/E+; CreativeI/iStock/Getty Images Plus; NadejdaReid/iStock/Getty Images Plus; standret/iStock/Getty Images Plus; Rhoberazzi/E+; S-S-S/iStock/Getty Images Plus; S-S-S/iStock/Getty Images Plus; LizaLutik/iStock/Getty Images Plus; Anna Erastova/iStock/Getty Images Plus; **U6:** Donald Iain Smith/Moment; sot/Photodisc; SDI Productions/E+; Jacobs Stock Photography Ltd/DigitalVision; Jupiterimages/Goodshoot; mediaphotos/iStock/Getty Images Plus; CasarsaGuru/E+; Tgordievskaya/iStock/Getty Images Plus; Robert Niedring/Cavan; Westend61; Mimi Haddon/DigitalVision; Nichola Sarah/Moment; Elva Etienne/Moment; Stefan Cristian Cioata/Moment; PraewBlackWhile/iStock/Getty Images Plus; Karen Brodie/Moment; Cezary Wojtkowski/iStock/Getty Images Plus; TomÃ¡s Pedreira/EyeEm; Hanna Plonsak/iStock/Getty Images Plus; CarlaNichiata/iStock/Getty Images Plus; Anna Erastova/iStock/Getty Images Plus; PeterSnow/iStock/Getty Images Plus; **U7:** Yura Yavorovich/iStock/Getty Images Plus; Klaus Hackenberg/The Image Bank; 10'000 Hours/DigitalVision BreakingTheWalls/iStock/Getty Images Plus; Joachim Berninger/EyeEm; Tom Baker/EyeEm; Helaine Weide/Moment; chris-mueller/iStock/Getty Images Plus; Katrin Ray Shumakov/Moment; YakubovAlim/iStock/Getty Images Plus; Jena Ardell/Moment; FatCamera/iStock/Getty Images Plus; NAKphotos/iStock/Getty Images Plus; Wavebreakmedia Ltd/Wavebreak Media; Lucidio Studio, Inc./Moment Open; Natalia-flurno/iStock/Getty Images Plus; Tetiana Lazunova/iStock/Getty Images Plus; Sentavio/iStock/Getty Images Plus; lukbar/iStock/Getty Images Plus; Anna Erastova/iStock/Getty Images Plus; Daria Pilshchikova/iStock/Getty Images Plus; Karuntana Chaiwatcharanun/iStock/Getty Images Plus; Maike Hildebrandt/iStock/Getty Images Plus; Liesel Bockl/fStop; Liesel Bockl/fStop; Picnote/iStockphoto/Getty Images; **U8:** Cultura RM Exclusive/Luc Beziat/Image Source; SDI Productions/E+; kali9/E+; xijian/E+; Caia Image/Collection Mix: Subjects; Siri Stafford/The Image Bank; Klaus Vedfelt/DigitalVision; stockvisual/E+; Iya Forbes/Moment; Jordan Lye/Moment; Yulia_Artemova/iStock/Getty Images Plus; seamartini/iStock/Getty Images Plus; Anna Erastova/iStock/Getty Images Plus; MuchMania/iStock/Getty Images Plus; PeterSnow/iStock/Getty Images Plus; Hanna Plonsak/iStock/Getty Images Plus; **V82:** Caia Image/Collection Mix: Subjects; **V83:** bortonia/DigitalVision Vectors; **V84:** Imgorthand/E+; Ryan McVay/DigitalVision; Studio Light and Shade/iStock/Getty Images Plus; Maskot; JGI/Jamie Grill/Tetra images; andresr/E+.

Cover photography by Tiffany Mumford for Creative Listening.

Commissioned photography by Stephen Noble and Duncan Yeldham for Creative Listening.

Illustrations

Ana Sebastian (Bright Agency); Dave Williams/Ryan Ball (roughs) (Bright Agency); David Belmont (Beehive); Javier Joaquin (Beehive); Laszlo Veres (Beehive); Moreno Chiacchiera (Beehive); Shahab (Sylvia Poggio).

Audio

Audio production by John Marshall Media.

Typeset

Blooberry Design

Additional authors

Rebecca Legros: CLIL
Montse Watkin: Sounds and life skills, Exam folder

Freelance editor

Melissa Bryant

Contents

High technology

1 Choose words from the box to complete the text.

> excited   going   laughed   math   something
> ~~started~~   terrible   thirtieth   won   year

The children (1) _____started_____ classes at school last week, and they're ready for another
(2) _____ of study. They're really (3) _____ about working on *Kid's Box* again,
their blog for young people. Last year they (4) _____ the school prize for the best blog,
and this year they want to enter an international blog competition to see if they can win again.
They're (5) _____ to visit a lot of places and write about some very interesting things.
Last Wednesday, they met to talk about their new project, and they also looked at some funny
photos from last year. They (6) _____ a lot when they remembered some of the things
that happened.

2 Correct the sentences.

1 The children started vacation last week. The children started classes at school last week.
2 They're ready for another month of study. _____
3 They won the school prize for art. _____
4 They met last Friday. _____
5 They watched some funny DVDs. _____
6 They cried a lot when they met. _____

3 What do you use these things for? Write sentences.

1 **2** **3**

4 **5** **6**

1 We use a toothbrush to brush our teeth.
2 _____
3 _____
4 _____
5 _____
6 _____

4 Answer the questions.

1 What did you do during vacation?
_____
2 Where did you go?
_____
3 Who did you see?
_____
4 What did you eat?
_____
5 What did you do?
_____
6 What was the weather like?
_____

Language: review of present tense   ▶ Do the online activities on **Practice Extra** as you complete this unit.

1 **Put the words in groups.**

bored   English   excited   ~~friendly~~   geography   happy   history
interested   ~~math~~   pepper   ~~pizza~~   salad   salt   sandwich   science

friendly
_____
_____
_____
_____

pizza
_____
_____
_____
_____

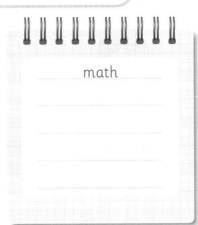

math
_____
_____
_____
_____

2 **Find the letters on the clock. Make words.**

1   It's twenty-five to twelve.   wing
2   It's twenty-five after six.   _____
3   It's twenty to four.   _____
4   It's ten after one.   _____
5   It's ten to nine.   _____

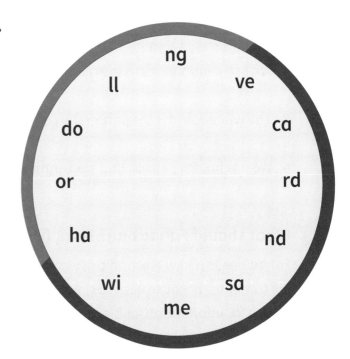

3 **Write times to make four more words.
You can use the same letters again.**

1   It's ten to eleven. (doll)
2   _____
3   _____
4   _____

4 **Find and write the adjectives.**

iped

ired   uge

errible   mous

appy   ong

~~mazing~~

amazing
a _____
fa _____
fa _____
da _____
da _____
s _____
s _____

h _____
h _____
lo _____
lo _____
str _____
str _____
t _____
t _____

ngerous

t   rk

ng   trong

oft

wake   ud

Look and complete the words.

1 v i d e o g a m e

2 m _ _ _ _ _ _ _ p h _ _ _ _

3 e _ _ _ _ _ _

4 h _ _ _ _ _ p h _ _ _

5 l _ _ t _ _ _

6 s _ _ _ _ _ s p _ _ _ _ _

 Find the mistakes. Write the correct sentences.

1 A laptop is a big heavy computer that we carry in a special bag.

A laptop is a small _____

2 We use headphones to see our friends when we chat with them.

_____

3 The whiteboard is the part of the computer we look at. We use it to watch videos.

_____

4 We use books, pencils, and smartphones to connect with people and programs online.

_____

 What should Fahad buy? Mark (✓) the correct box.

Fahad needs a new electronic device because his computer is very old. He has a lot of problems with his computer because it is too slow. He wants a fast internet connection because he often needs to search for information for his school projects and upload his homework. He also likes to chat with his friends online, but he never plays games. He wants an electronic device he can carry when he travels and that he can use to take pictures and videos. The screen needs to be a large size to look at the pictures and videos. He also wants a keyboard that is easy to use and isn't very small.

In your notebook, write three reasons why you chose that electronic device.

 Vocabulary: technology

1 Join two words to make one. Write the new word.

1	home	ball	
2	head	line	
3	on	room	
4	class	work	homework
5	basket	phones	

2 Write another word at the end to make new words.

1 bathroom   3 ear   5 arm   7 white

2 book   4 lap   6 tooth   8 snow

3   Find and say eight differences. Then write sentences.

In picture "a," the girl's chatting online. In picture "b," she's watching a movie.

4 Answer the questions.

1 How do you go online?

2 Do you write emails?

3 Do you use apps to chat with your friends?

4 Do you have a smart speaker at home?

5 Do you upload your homework with an app?

6 Do you play online video games with your friends?

7 How do you listen to music?

8 Do you prefer laptops, tablets, or smartphones?

Sounds and life skills
Being a good school citizen
Pronunciation focus

1 🎧 2 **Listen and circle the stressed part of the words.**

1 compe(ti)tion   5 laptop
2 computer   6 tablet
3 exciting   7 technology
4 internet

2 🎧 3 **Complete with the words from Activity 1. Listen and check.**

1 Oo	2 Ooo	3 oOo	4 oOoo	5 ooOo
				competition

3 🎧 4 **Listen and number the pictures.**

4 **Read and complete.** arrive   do   help   keep   ~~take~~   take

How to be a good school citizen

We have to ...

take our library books to the library.   _____ our classmates.
_____ to class on time.   _____ our homework.
_____ our classroom clean.   _____ care of the technology we use.

  Sounds and life skills: stressed words | 🛡 social responsibilities

1 Read and answer.

Diggory Bones

1 What time's Diggory giving his talk? At half past two.
2 What kind of computer does Diggory have? _____
3 What can he use to explain ancient math and technology? _____
4 Who's Sir Doug Bones? _____
5 Why does he want to look under the cloth? _____
6 Who has the calendar at the end? _____

2 Look at the code. Write the secret message.

a	b	c	d	e	f	g	h	i	j	k	l	m

n	o	p	q	r	s	t	u	v	w	x	y	z

T h e _____

_____ .

Do you remember?

1 10:55 is five   to   eleven.
2 _____ don't we buy a new computer?
3 I play online _____ with my friends all over the world.
4 A small computer that we can carry easily is a _____ .
5 _____ and _____ are two words with the stress pattern Oo.
6 One word with the stress pattern oOoo is _____ .

Can do

I can make and agree to suggestions.

I can talk about technology.

I can write about my school.

1 Beastly tales

STUDY AGAIN — Going to

We use *going to* to talk about plans.

Affirmative	Negative	Question
I'm **going to** read.	You **aren't going to** listen to music.	**Is** he **going to** play tennis?
She's **going to** read.	We **aren't going to** listen to music.	**Are** they **going to** play tennis?
We're **going to** read.	He **isn't going to** listen to music.	**Am** I **going to** play tennis?

 1 Correct the questions and answer.

1 Am you going to be in the school play? Are you going to be in the school play? No, I'm not.

2 Do your dad going to cook dinner tonight? _____

3 Are you go to watch a movie after school? _____

4 Has your mom going to go to the theater this weekend? _____

5 What is your friends going to do on the weekend? _____

6 Does your teacher going to give you homework today? _____

2 Complete the questions. Match them to the answers.

> **What   When   Where   ~~Which~~   Who   Why**

1 _Which_ bus are you going to catch?   a He's going to call his mom. ☐
2 _____ are we going to play soccer?   b They're going to take it tomorrow. ☐
3 _____ is he going to call?   c He's going to read his comic book. ☐
4 _____ is she going to wash the car?   d I'm going to catch the number 27. ☐1
5 _____ is he going to read?   e In the park. ☐
6 _____ are they going to take the test?   f Because it's dirty. ☐

 3 Look at the code. Write the secret message.

H	I	J	K	L	M	N	O	P	Q	R	S	T	U	V	W	X	Y	Z	A	B	C	D	E	F	G
A	B	C	D	E	F	G	H	I	J	K	L	M	N	O	P	Q	R	S	T	U	V	W	X	Y	Z

A O L   A O L H A L Y   J S B I   P Z   N V P U N   A V   Z O V D   A O L   W S H F
T h e

V U   A O L   S H Z A   A O B Y Z K H F   H U K   M Y P K H F   V M   Q B U L .
.

Language: plans, intentions, and predictions with *going to*

Do the online activities on **Practice Extra** as you complete this unit.

Find six sentences or questions and write them in your notebook.

He isn't	tickets do you	other animals.
How many	to get parts in	tomorrow.
Are they going	going to be	monkey.
They didn't	isn't going to rain	an actor.
Lions	choose him for the	the play?
It	catch and eat	want?

 What are they going to do?

1 Hiroto's turning on the TV.
   He's going to watch TV.

2 Lola's standing outside the castle, and she's holding her camera.

3 The car's very dirty. Mr. White is walking toward it with some water.

4 Some people are standing at the bus stop.

5 The boys are walking to the park. They're carrying a soccer ball.

6 There's some paper in front of Petra, and she's picking up a pen.

 Think about next year. Write notes to answer the questions.

1 How old are you going to be? _____

2 What grade are you going to be in at school? _____

3 Which subjects are you going to study? _____

4 Which clubs are you going to join? _____

5 What are you going to do after school and on which days? _____

6 Which books are you going to read? _____

7 Which movies are you going to see? _____

8 What else are you going to do? _____

 Use your answers to write sentences about what you're going to do next year.

In January next year, I'm going to be

Find the words. Label the picture.

f	a	i	r	i	e	n
n	e	s	t	o	s	h
a	a	a	u	e	c	o
o	g	g	t	e	a	r
e	l	a	o	h	l	n
f	e	e	o	u	e	f
c	l	a	w	u	s	r

1 ___eagle___

2 _____

3 _____

4 _____

5 _____

6 _____

 Look at the picture and correct the sentences.

1 The dragon has fur on its body. The dragon has scales on its body. _____

2 The dragon wants to get the parrot's eggs. _____

3 The dragon and the eagle have dangerous hands. _____

4 The dragon has feathers on its wings, but the eagle doesn't. _____

5 The dragon has two ears on its head. _____

6 The eagle's eggs are in a cave. _____

3 📝 **Look at these beasts. Invent names and describe them.**

1

2

3

This is a "Dinobear."
It has a dinosaur's
_____
_____
_____
_____

_____
_____
_____
_____
_____

_____
_____
_____
_____
_____

Read and answer "yes" or "no."

The Sphinx existed in ancient Egyptian and ancient Greek mythology. In Greek mythology, the Sphinx had a lion's body, legs, and claws, a snake's tail, an eagle's wings, and a woman's head. The story says that she sat at the door of the ancient city of Thebes to guard it. To go into the city, people had to answer the Sphinx's question. If they got it right, they could go into the city. If they got it wrong, she ate them. The Ancient Greek writer, Sophocles, wrote the question in his work. It was "What creature goes on four feet in the morning, two feet in the afternoon and three feet in the evening?" Do you know the answer?

1 The Sphinx was a real animal. _no_
2 She had a bird's wings. _____
3 She had a mammal's tail. _____
4 She stood at the door of Thebes. _____
5 She asked people a question. _____
6 People who didn't know went home. _____

 Write the words.

1 an ancient story about heroes = _myth_
2 snakes have these on their bodies = _____
3 birds have these on their wings = _____
4 a word for an animal or creature = _____
5 a very expensive yellow metal = _____
6 some birds make these in trees = _____
7 half man, half horse = _____
8 half woman, half fish = _____

 What's going to happen?

The boat is going to hit
the rocks.

_____

_____

_____

_____

_____

Sounds and life skills

Supporting your friends

Pronunciation focus

1 🎧 5 **Listen and write.**
1 r _ _ _ _   3 p _ _ _ _   5 _ _ _ _ _ _   7 _ _ _ _
2 b r _ _ _   4 w _ _ _ _   6 _ _ _ _ _ _

2 🎧 6 **Listen and complete. Practice saying the sentences.**

| acting   exciting   going   interesting   ~~singing~~   starting   Writing |

1 I'm good at _____singing_____ , but I'm not good at _____ .
2 I love _____ to the theater!
3 I'm _____ guitar lessons after school today.
4 I think dragons are _____ , but they're also a little scary.
5 _____ a blog isn't always easy, but it's _____ .

3 **Read and match.**

1 I'm worried about my test
2 I'm starting sailing lessons,
3 I'm good at singing on stage,
4 I'm going to play in my first soccer game,

a but I'm terrible at scoring goals.
b but I get very nervous in front of a lot of people.
c because I get very nervous and forget things!
d and I'm worried because I'm not a good swimmer.

4 **Read and complete the advice. Then match to a situation in Activity 3.**

| can   Go   good   Good   luck   ~~worry~~ |

a Don't _____worry_____ . You're _____ at singing! Close your eyes and enjoy the songs! ☐

b You're on vacation! Why not start swimming lessons at the same time? _____ for it! ☐

c It's fantastic you are on the soccer team! _____ job! Practice scoring your goals with a friend on the weekend. ☐

d You _____ do it! Talk about the topic with a friend or your family. Relax and go to bed early the night before. Good _____ ! ☐

1 Read and answer.

Diggory Bones

1 Where's the Aztec calendar from? It's from a museum in Mexico City.
2 Who's Iyam Greedy? _____
3 How do you write 6 in the Mayan math system? _____
4 Who was Quetzalcóatl? _____
5 What's in the email? _____
6 Where are Diggory and Emily going to go? _____

2 Complete and match.

1 How am I _____going to_____ tell the museum in Mexico City? [d]

2 A spot means one, and _____ five. ☐

3 It _____ a phone number to me. ☐

4 I'm a snake, and I _____ . ☐

5 He was _____ and part snake. ☐

Do you remember?

1 They aren't _____going_____ to choose Sally for the part of the monkey.
2 They are going _____ write about exciting beasts.
3 Dragons have _____ on their bodies.
4 Eagles live in _____ in high places.
5 _____ is the day before Friday and the day after Wednesday.
6 There are _____ days in the weekend.

Can do

I can talk about what is going to happen.

I can talk about beasts from myths and legends.

I can write about mythical beasts.

How have our toys and games changed?

1 **Read and complete with "who" and "that."**

Everybody loves

J e n g a

Leslie Scott is the name of the British board-game designer (1) _____who_____ created Jenga in the 1970s. The game begins with a tower (2) _____ has 54 blocks. Players have to take the blocks away from the tower without making it fall, and then put the blocks on top of it.

The game needs two or more players. The winner is the player (3) _____ does not make the tower fall. It's a game (4) _____ takes between five and 15 minutes to play.

The name Jenga comes from *kujenga*, a Swahili word (5) _____ means "to build."

Jenga is a game without a board, but I believe that everyone (6) _____ loves board games will also love Jenga!

2 **Plan to write a review. Complete the table for a game you enjoy.**

My Review	
Paragraph 1 What's the game?	_____ is a _____ game that _____. The winner is the player who _____.
Paragraph 2 How do you play the game?	The game has _____. Players use _____ to _____. It's a game that usually takes _____ minutes.
Paragraph 3 How many players do you need?	To play _____, you need _____ players. Players should be between _____ years old. That makes it a perfect game for _____.
Paragraph 4 What do you think?	I believe every family should have _____ because _____.

3 📝 **Use your notes to write your game review.**

4 **Did you ...**

- ☐ plan your game review?
- ☐ use interesting words to describe the game?
- ☐ give your own opinion?
- ☐ read your game review again?
- ☐ check grammar, spelling, and punctuation?

Writing tip

Writing a game review

When you write a game review, you should give some facts about the game, but you can also say what you like and what you don't like.

Clue is a game **that** ...

I think Clue is a great game because ...

Flyers Listening

STUDY AGAIN   will

We use *will* to talk about predictions for the future.

Affirmative	Negative	Question
I'll go to the moon.	You **won't** travel by car.	**Will** she fly in a rocket?
It'll go to the moon.	We **won't** travel by car.	**Will** they fly in a rocket?

1   Read and match.

1 We will have   a invent a carplane.
2 She won't go   b will go to the moon on vacation.
3 He will go to   c online classes every day. `1`
4 There won't be any   d work by rocket.
5 Someone will   e to school by bus.
6 Some people   f cars in a hundred years.

2   Complete the table. Mark (✓) "Yes" or "No."

Will you ...	Yes	No
1 travel to the moon?		
2 have the same job as your parents?		
3 have a lot of pets?		
4 live in the same town as you live in now?		
5 go to college when you're older?		

3 **Now write sentences with "will" or "won't."**

I will / won't travel to the moon.

1 _____
2 _____
3 _____
4 _____
5 _____

4 **Read the notes. Complete the sentences.**

9:00	Arrive at school. Change clothes for P.E.
9:15	Play badminton.
10:00	Take a shower.
10:30	Go to math class.
11:15	Go out to play. Drink some orange juice.

1 When Peter arrives at school, he'll change his clothes for P.E.

2 After he plays badminton, _____

3 After he has math class, _____

4 When he goes out to play, _____

▸ Do the online activities on **Practice Extra** as you complete this unit.

1 Will these things happen in 2075? Write sentences with "will" or "won't."

1 Children / classes / home   Children won't have classes at home.

2 People / go / Mars _____

3 People / fly / cars _____

4 People / use smartphones _____

5 Children / do sports outside _____

6 People / use less plastic _____

 2 Read and complete.

arms   brush   cup   quickly   ~~shower~~   will   won't

This is my new invention to help children in the future. It's a cross between a (1) ___shower___ and a car wash. It'll have two funny metal (2) _____ with big gloves made of rubber. These (3) _____ move around and around very (4) _____ to wash us with soap and water. One of them will (5) _____ our teeth with a toothbrush, too. Outside the shower, there'll be a machine with an engine to dry us. It'll look like a big (6) _____ that we'll stand under. We'll take a shower, and we (7) _____ have a wet towel.

 3 Design and draw an invention to help children in the future.

4 Write about your invention.

Label the pictures.   astronaut   businessperson   Earth   engineer   rocket   ~~tourist~~

tourist

 Complete the sentences.

1 ____Space____ is the name we give to everything outside Earth's atmosphere.

2 An _____ is a person who designs or makes machines or electrical things.

3 We breathe _____ .

4 The planet _____ is where we live.

5 An _____ can travel in space.

6 The _____ goes around our planet. We can see it at night.

7 A _____ visits another town or country on vacation.

8 Someone who works in business is called a _____ .

9 A _____ travels very quickly and can take people into space.

 Read and answer "yes" or "no."

The Space Race started in 1957 when the Soviet Union sent a satellite called Sputnik 1 into space. A satellite is something that goes around Earth. The U.S.A. sent a satellite called Explorer 1 into space in 1958. Eleven years later, American astronaut Neil Armstrong became the first person to walk on the moon. Now, we can explore farther into space with robots instead of people. In July 2020, NASA sent a robot called Perseverance to Mars. It carried a small helicopter with it to take pictures. Mars is very far away from Earth. Perseverance didn't land on Mars until February 2021!

1 The first satellite in space was called Sputnik 1. yes

2 The U.S.A. sent a satellite into space in 1959. _____

3 Neil Armstrong was the first man to walk on the moon. _____

4 NASA sent astronauts to Mars in 2020. _____

5 Perseverance took a small helicopter with it. _____

6 Perseverance landed on Mars in 2020. _____

Match the ideas about life in Zeron, the space city. Write sentences.

1	telescopes in the windows	a	to build new houses
2	satellites	b	to get energy
3	solar panels	c	to travel into space
4	robots	d	to look at the stars
5	rockets	e	to receive signals from space

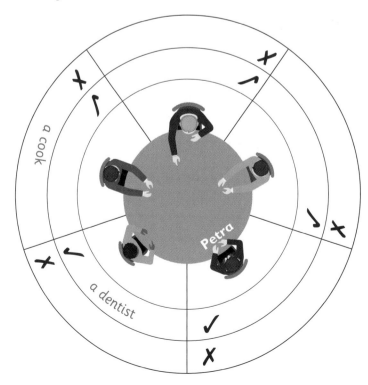

1 We'll have telescopes in the windows to look at the stars.

2 _____

3 _____

4 _____

5 _____

 Read and solve the riddles.

1 The beginning of Earth, the end of space. The beginning of every end, the end of every place. What am I? _____ "e"_____

2 What comes once in a minute, twice in a moment, and never in a thousand years? _____

3 Which letter will come next in this sequence? M, A, M, J, J, A, S, O … ? _____

4 How will you use the letters in NEW DOOR to make one word? _____

5 Akash was an engineer. His mother had four children. The first was April, the second was May, and the third was June. What was the name of her fourth child? _____

6 A man's looking at a photo of a famous astronaut and says, "I have no brothers and sisters, but that man's father is my father's son." Who's he looking at? _____

 Read and complete the circle with names and jobs.

There are three girls and two boys. They're talking about the jobs they think they will (✓) and won't (✗) do in the future.

1 Petra's sitting between Quinn and Lucas. The person on Lucas's left thinks she'll be an actor, but she won't be a painter.

2 The boy who says he'll be a dentist won't be an actor.

3 The person on Mary's left won't be a photographer, but she thinks she'll be a mechanic.

4 The girl next to Lucy loves cameras, so she'll be a photographer, but she won't be a cook.

5 The boy next to Lucy loves rockets, but he won't be an astronaut. He thinks he'll be a rocket engineer.

Sounds and life skills
Choosing a point of view

Pronunciation focus

1 🎧 8 **Listen and underline the stress in the verbs.**

In 2100, …

1 People will <u>trav</u>el to the moon on vacation.
2 Field trips will visit space.
3 We'll ride bicycles that can fly.
4 Students won't have paper textbooks.
5 Everyone will wear a computer on their arm.
6 People won't shop at supermarkets.

2 **Read the rules and circle "weak" or "strong."**

We don't say every word in a sentence with the same stress. The strong words give important information. When we make the important words stronger, it's easier for people to understand.

1 Verbs, adjectives, and nouns are usually **weak / strong**.
2 Helping verbs (*will, can, should*) are usually **weak / strong**.
3 Negative words (*won't, don't, didn't*) are usually **weak / strong**.

> We'll **travel** by **fast cars**, but they **won't** use **gas**.

3 🎧 9 **Listen. What does Nico think? Mark (✓) "Agree" or "Disagree."**

	Agree	Disagree
1 moon vacations	✓	
2 field trips to space		
3 flying bicycles		
4 no paper textbooks		
5 computers on arms		
6 no supermarket shopping		

4 **Circle your point of view. Then complete with a reason.**

1 In 2100, I **agree / disagree** that people will travel to the moon for their vacations because

_____.

2 In 2100, I **agree / disagree** that field trips will visit space because

_____.

3 In 2100, I **agree / disagree** that we'll ride bicycles that can fly because

_____.

4 In 2100, I **agree / disagree** that students won't have paper textbooks because

_____.

5 In 2100, I **agree / disagree** that everyone will wear a computer on their arm because

_____.

6 In 2100, I **agree / disagree** that people won't shop at supermarkets because

_____.

Diggory Bones

1 Read and answer.

1 Why did Iyam Greedy send them tickets to Mexico City? There are legends about Aztec gold.
2 What did the Aztecs and the Mayas use to measure time? _____
3 When did the Aztec new year start? _____
4 What will be the longest day of the year? _____
5 What's the date now in the story? _____
6 Will they stay in Mexico City tonight? _____

2 Read and order the text. Write the story in your notebook.

technology and their ancient math system. Iyam Greedy, who's a pirate and ☐

notebook and talked about a group of stars. There was a man sitting next to them. He ☐

phone number for Diggory in a letter. When Diggory called the number, Iyam ☐

only wants to get the Aztec gold and be rich, stole the Sun Stone and left a ☐

Diggory Bones is an archeologist who teaches at City University. He had the ☐ 1

On the plane to Mexico City, Diggory and his daughter, Emily, looked at a ☐

man from the plane got into a car with Iyam Greedy and followed their bus. ☐

listened to them talking. When Diggory and Emily caught a bus to Teotihuacán, the ☐

talked about Aztec mythology. Then he sent him two plane tickets in an email. ☐

Sun Stone. That is the name for the Aztec calendar, which he had to talk about Mayan (and Aztec) ☐

Do you remember?

1 In the future, there _____will_____ be spaceplanes.
2 That's not a very good paper plane. It _____ fly very far.
3 _____ are people who fly in space for their job.
4 Our planet is called _____ .
5 In the question "When'll they arrive?" "'ll" is a contraction of _____ .
6 _____ they build a spaceplane for tourists, we'll fly around Earth for our vacation.

Can do

I can talk about what will happen.

I can talk about travel in the future.

I can write about how we'll live in the future.

What can robots do for us?

1 **Read and order. Then circle the instruction verbs.**

MY SCHOOL PROJECT

Draw a simple design of your robot. Decide what
materials you will need. ☐ 1

Finally, color the robot's body and decorate its face. ☐

Test the robot to check it won't break. ☐

Build your robot with the materials. ☐

Find the materials you need to build your robot. ☐

2 **Plan to write instructions. Complete the table about how to make a robot. Use the instruction verbs from the box.**

> Bring   build   Choose   ~~decide~~   decorate   Draw   Paint   plan   Write

Type of robot	How to make a _____.
Instructions	First, ____decide____ what type of robot to make.
	Then _____ your robot. Think about what it will look like and what you will need.
	_____ a picture of what your robot will look like.
	_____ the materials you will need. _____ them down in your notebook.
	Now _____ your robot carefully with your materials. If something doesn't work, try again!
	_____ and _____ your robot with colors. Look at your picture again to help you.
	_____ your robot to school and show your friends!

3 **Use your notes to write your instructions.**

4 **Did you ...**

☐ plan your instructions?

☐ use instruction verbs?

☐ read your instructions again?

☐ check grammar, spelling, and punctuation?

Writing tip

Writing instructions

Instructions should start with the first thing you need to do. They should end with the last thing you need to do. Use words like *choose*, *plan*, *draw*, *build*, *paint*, and *color* to show how to make something.

Flyers Reading and Writing

1 **Look and read. Choose the correct words and write them on the lines.**
There is one example.

rockets   **a monkey**   a theater   stars

a camera

| You use this to take pictures. It isn't a smartphone. | *a camera* |

a lion

1 A big road where people can drive fast. _____

2 Astronauts use these to fly into space. _____

3 This is a person who flies a plane. _____

a mouse

4 This day comes after Wednesday. _____

an island

5 This animal is a very big cat. It's called "the king of the beasts." _____

planets

6 This is a piece of land in the ocean. There's water all around it. _____

a driver

7 This is the place where you go to see a play. _____

8 There are a lot of these in the sky. You can see them clearly at night. _____

gold

a stadium

9 There are eight of these in our solar system. _____

10 This yellow metal is very expensive. People make rings and bracelets from it. _____

a pilot   Thursday   trees   a highway

Review Units 1 and 2

1 **Read the story. Choose a word from the box. Write the correct word next to numbers 1–8.**

actor   cook   designer   drive   engineer   ~~favorite~~   food
future   house   museum   picture   rocket   tomorrow   will   won't

FRIENDLY

Friendly is Sally, Eva, and Robert's ___favorite___ TV show. It's a comedy, and it's very funny. It's about five friends who all live and study in the same school. Last week, the friends had an interview with a special teacher to talk about their (1) _____ jobs. They had to think about which school subjects they were good at and where they wanted to work.

Frankie wants to study art in college. Jim loves sports and staying healthy and wants to be a firefighter. Peter loves (2) _____, and he says he'll be a cook. Sally says she'll be a taxi driver. Jenny's good at English and drama and wants to be an (3) _____. She says that when she's famous, Sally (4) _____ drive her to the movie studio, Peter will (5) _____ her delicious meals, and Frankie will paint a (6) _____ of her and put it in a big, important (7) _____. When Jim asks what he'll do for her, Jenny says her (8) _____ will never catch fire, so he'll have to change jobs!

2 **Choose a title for this episode of *Friendly*.**

Mark (✓) one box.   Past and present ☐   After-school club ☐   Future plans ☐

3 **Read the jokes. Match the questions to the answers.**

1 What's green and smells like paint?
2 How does a monster count to 13?
3 Which side of an eagle has the most feathers?
4 What do you get if you cross a blue cat with a red parrot?
5 How many seconds are there in a year?
6 What animal can jump higher than a house?
7 Where can you find an ocean without water?
8 Why don't mother kangaroos like rainy days?
9 What goes through towns and up and over hills, but doesn't move?
10 What do you get if you cross a parrot with a tiger?

a The outside. ☐
b All of them can. A house can't jump. ☐
c A purple carrot! ☐
d I don't know, but when it talks you should listen carefully! ☐
e Green paint. 1
f On its fingers! ☐
g A road. ☐
h On a map! ☐
i Twelve: January the second, February the second … ☐
j Because their children have to play inside! ☐

4 Complete the sentences. Count and write the letters.

1 _____Space_____ is the place outside Earth's atmosphere, where the moon and planets are. ⑤

2 A griffin's nest is made of _____. ☐

3 Wi-Fi, smart speakers, TVs, headphones, and the internet are all examples of _____. ☐

4 We breathe _____. It's called "wind" when it moves over Earth. ☐

5 Somebody who works in space is an _____. ☐

6 Eagles have a lot of _____ on their wings. ☐

7 A small, light computer that we can carry easily is a _____. ☐

8 "What _____ you do?" "I'll ask Hiroto to help me." ☐

9 The sun is the only _____ in our solar system. ☐

10 The _____ is the part of the computer that has the letters which we use to write. ☐

11 A space station uses a _____ to send astronauts into space. ☐

12 An _____ designs cars and motorcycles. ☐

13 We send an _____ to our friends using the internet. ☐

14 _____ are at the end of a dragon's leg. ☐

5 Now complete the crossword. Write the message.

(crossword grid with numbered clues 1–10 and message boxes)

Message boxes: 1 2 3 4 | 5 6 | 7 8 9 10 [S] !

6 Quiz time!

1 What part did Sally play in the audition? The naughty monkey.

2 Who did Jason sail with? _____

3 Where did people play senet? _____

4 How will tourists fly into space in the future? _____

5 What do astronauts need to live in space for a long time? _____

6 How fast can Raptor the robot run? _____

7 📝 Write questions for your quiz in your notebook.

3 The great outdoors

Past progressive

We use the past progressive to describe what was happening in the past.

Affirmative	Negative	Question
I **was climbing** when I fell.	I **wasn't walking**.	**Was** I **playing**?
You **were climbing** when you fell.	He **wasn't walking**.	**Was** she **playing**?
He **was climbing** when he fell.	They **weren't walking**.	**Were** we **playing**?

1 Read and match.

1 She was skating
2 We were cooking sausages
3 You were flying your kite
4 He was skiing down the hill fast
5 I was sleeping
6 They were waiting at the station

when

a he saw a tree in front of him.
b it flew into a tree.
c she fell down.
d the kitchen caught fire.
e their train arrived.
f you called me.

☐
☐
1
☐
☐
☐

2 Look at the pictures. Answer the questions.

1 Was Richard playing volleyball at quarter after eleven? Yes, he was.

2 Were Tanaz and George doing their homework at quarter after five? _____

3 Was Hiroto playing the guitar at ten after seven? _____

4 Were Kito and Yu Xi having lunch at twenty-five after one? _____

5 Was Sophia brushing her teeth at half past eight? _____

6 Were Nadia and Oliver watching TV at ten to five? _____

3 Complete the sentences for you.

1 Yesterday I was going to school when _____

2 When I was eating my breakfast this morning, _____

3 My friends were playing on the weekend when _____

4 When our teacher was talking, _____

1 Match the sentences to the pictures.

1 We looked at our map. We had to walk through a forest to get to the campsite.

2 In this picture, we were eating the sandwiches that George and Harry got from the café. We couldn't eat the sausages because they were burned black!

3 Last week, I went camping with my friends George and Harry. When we got off the bus, it was raining.

4 Our feet were hurting after the long walk, and we were tired and hungry when we arrived.

5 It was getting late when we were walking through the forest, and it was very dark.

6 This is a picture of me when I was cooking the sausages. I'm not a very good cook.

2 Read and answer "yes" or "no."

1 He went camping with his friends Harry and George.   yes

2 It was raining when they got off the bus. _____

3 They had to walk up a hill to get to the campsite. _____

4 The sun was coming up when they were walking through the forest. _____

5 Their feet were hurting when they arrived at the campsite. _____

6 When he was cooking the sausages, he burned them. _____

3 Read and answer.

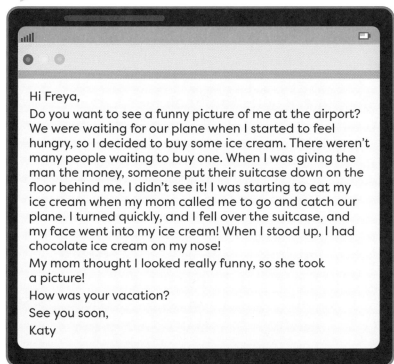

Hi Freya,

Do you want to see a funny picture of me at the airport? We were waiting for our plane when I started to feel hungry, so I decided to buy some ice cream. There weren't many people waiting to buy one. When I was giving the man the money, someone put their suitcase down on the floor behind me. I didn't see it! I was starting to eat my ice cream when my mom called me to go and catch our plane. I turned quickly, and I fell over the suitcase, and my face went into my ice cream! When I stood up, I had chocolate ice cream on my nose!

My mom thought I looked really funny, so she took a picture!

How was your vacation?

See you soon,

Katy

1 What were Katy and her mom doing at the airport? They were waiting for the plane.

2 Were there many people waiting to buy ice cream? _____

3 When did someone put their suitcase down behind her? _____

4 What was she starting to do when her mom called her? _____

5 What did her mom think when she stood up? _____

Look at the picture. Find the words (a–l) in the wordsearch.

s	m	o	u	n	t	a	i	n	y	r
l	e	r	f	n	c	w	e	s	t	f
e	b	c	e	o	n	t	k	t	g	l
e	a	h	e	s	r	n	o	s	t	a
p	c	s	n	k	t	e	n	t	i	s
i	t	a	t	a	z	y	s	a	l	h
n	o	e	m	p	n	r	e	t	l	l
g	u	e	x	p	l	o	r	e	r	i
b	c	s	q	i	u	g	r	l	a	g
a	h	t	n	x	s	o	u	t	h	h
g	b	a	c	k	p	a	c	k	h	t

2 **Write the words. Then write the letters from Activity 1.**

1   _camp_   = to live and sleep outdoors   `a`
2   _____   = a bag you can sleep in   ☐
3   _____   = the opposite of "north"   ☐
4   _____   = something you can use to see when it's dark   ☐
5   _____   = a high place that's higher than a hill   ☐
6   _____   = a place where you can sleep   ☐

3 **Write definitions for three more words in Activity 1. Then write the letters.**

_____   ☐
_____   ☐
_____   ☐

4 📝 **Look at the code. Write the secret message in your notebook.**

> N = north   E = east   S = south   W = west

When – 5E – 4N – 2W – 3S – 2W – 1N – 3E – 2S – 4N – 2W – 3S – 2W – 2N – 5E – 1S – 2W – 2S – 2W – 1E – 2N – 2W – 2N – 1E – 1S – 2E – 1W – 2E – 2S – 1E.

a	warm,	carry	hiking	always	are
You	dry	and	jacket,	a	should
fruit,	mountains,	some	a	you	take
backpack.	the	a	in	cell	phone.
When	of	water,	bottle	should	you

Read the sentences. Draw and write on the map.

 The New Forest is 5 km north of Starton.

 The mountains are 3 km east of the New Forest.

 There's a bridge over the river 5 km west of the New Forest.

 2 km south of the mountains, there's a hotel. Its name is the Happy Inn.

 There's a lake 5 km west of Starton. It's called Emerald Lake.

 Hampton is 2 km north of Emerald Lake.

 The campsite is 3 km east of Hampton.

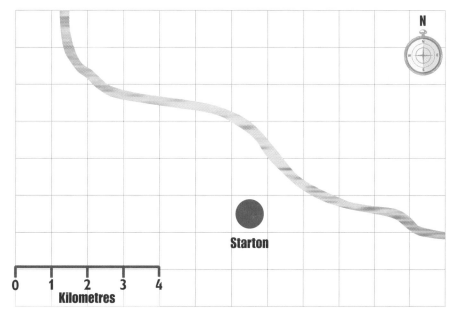

Starton

0   1   2   3   4
Kilometres

 Now draw these things on the map in Activity 1. Write the directions.

The flashlight is _____.

The backpack is _____.

The umbrella is _____.

The suitcase is _____.

3 **Find the letters on the clock. Write the words.**

1 It's quarter to eight.   south

2 It's five after ten.   _____

3 It's twenty-five after eight.   _____

4 It's quarter after six.   _____

5 It's twenty after ten.   _____

 In your notebook, write times to make four more words.

Sounds and life skills
Imagining possibilities

Pronunciation focus

1 🎧 10 **Listen and write the words under /b/, /v/, or /w/.**

/b/	/v/	/w/
bridge		

2 🎧 11 **Complete with words from Activity 1. Listen and check.**

1 Look! There's a _____ bike _____ on the _____ !

2 Let's _____ in the _____ . It's a beautiful day.

3 Why don't we _____ a _____ ? It's very cold outside.

4 We always _____ my aunt Vicky on Wednesdays.

5 Oh, no! My _____ fell in the river _____ we were looking at the _____ !

3 🎧 12 **Order the sentences. Listen and check.**

1 walking / river / fast / We / were / over a / when I fell in.
   We were walking over a fast river when I fell in.

2 walking / bridge / were / We / on a / when I fell and broke my leg.
   _____

3 were / in the / We / woods / walking / when I broke my leg.
   _____

4 near a / beautiful / walking / were / We / waterfall / when I fell.
   _____

4 **How did they break their arm? Look and complete.** (jump ride run)

1 I was _____ when I broke my arm!

2 _____ when I broke my arm!

3 _____ when I broke my arm!

1 Read and answer.

Diggory Bones

1 Who was getting out of the car behind them? Richard Tricker was getting out of the car.

2 Where's the Temple of Quetzalcóatl? _____

3 How far is Mexico City from the hotel? _____

4 Why does the man know about this place? _____

5 What does the long street join? _____

6 Was Diggory expecting to see Iyam there? _____

2 Put the verbs into the correct past tense.

The story of Mexico City

In about 1325, some young Aztecs (1) __were getting__ (are getting) food for their people when they (2) _____ (see) an eagle. It (3) _____ (is sitting) on a plant that (4) _____ (is growing) on a small island in the middle of a lake called Texcoco. They (5) _____ (think) it (6) _____ (is) a special sign, and they (7) _____ (decide) to build their city there.

The Aztecs (8) _____ (are) great engineers. They (9) _____ (take) water out of the lake to make the islands bigger. They (10) _____ (build) canals, so people (11) _____ (can) move around the city by boat, and bridges, which they (12) _____ (take) away at night to protect their city. They (13) _____ (call) their city Tenochtitlán, and it (14) _____ (become) one of the biggest and most important cities in the world at that time. The Aztecs (15) _____ (are) very rich because they (16) _____ (have) land, farms, markets, and stores. They (17) _____ (use) the Mayan number system and calendar, and they (18) _____ (study) the stars and the night sky carefully. Like the ancient Egyptians, they (19) _____ (write) with pictures on a kind of paper. The name of the Aztec people at the time (20) _____ (is) "the Mexica."

Do you remember?

1 What ____were____ you doing at six o'clock yesterday?

2 I was _____ TV.

3 When I go camping, I sleep in a _____ in my tent.

4 Marco Polo traveled _____ from China to Italy.

5 The teacher was talking _____ the door opened.

6 The street joins the Pyramid of the _____ and the Pyramid of the Moon.

Can do

I can use the past progressive tense to talk about the past.

I can talk about the outdoors and follow directions.

I can write directions to places in the outdoors.

What can we see in our world?

1 **Read and complete with the correct form of the verbs.**

Marcus Rashford

Marcus Rashford is a famous English soccer player. I admire him because he's a great player, but also because he likes (1) _____helping_____ (help) others.

Marcus was born in Manchester on October 31, 1997. As a child, he loved (2) _____ (play) soccer. The Manchester United schoolboys club chose him as their youngest player ever when he was 11 years old. It was a challenge because he played with older boys, but he achieved great success.

I think Marcus is a good person because he likes (3) _____ (use) his position as a famous soccer player to help children in need. He's achieved so much on and off the soccer field, and he'd like (4) _____ (write) a book because he'd like (5) _____ (help) children read.

I'd like (6) _____ (achieve) something like Marcus one day because he's a great person. I think it's important to be a role model for young people.

2 **Plan to write a profile. Complete the table for a person you admire.**

Who is it?	_____ is a/an _____ .
Why do you admire him/her?	I admire him/her because _____ .
Where was he/she born and when?	He/She was born in _____ on _____ .
What did he/she do at school?	At school, he/she _____ .
What was challenging for him/her?	_____ was a challenge, but _____ .
What do you think about his/her achievement?	I think _____ .
What is he/she doing now?	He/She still _____ .
What would you like to achieve one day?	I'd like/love to _____ .

3 **Use your notes to write your profile.**

4 **Did you …**

- ☐ plan your profile?
- ☐ write about the person's achievements?
- ☐ describe what they like doing and would like to do?
- ☐ read your profile again?
- ☐ check grammar, spelling, and punctuation?

Writing tip

Writing a profile

Give a lot of different information about a person to make it interesting. You can say the place and the year they were born, what they like to do, and what they would like to do in the future.

Flyers Listening

1 🎧 13 **Listen and write. There is one example.**

The vacation camp

Name of camp:	The Lake Camp	
1	Price:	_____ dollars a night
2	When:	_____ to October 10
3	Name of lake:	_____
4	Take:	_____
5	Camp phone number:	_____

4 Food, glorious food!

STUDY AGAIN | Countable and uncountable nouns

Countable nouns	Uncountable nouns
We can count them: strawberries, olives …	We can't count them: water, bread …
There **aren't enough** chairs.	There **isn't enough** water.
There **are too many** people.	There**'s too much** bread.

1 Follow the uncountable food words.

breakfast	pear	strawberry	potato chips	egg	fries	lunch	lime
orange	burger	fruit juice	chocolate	lemonade	soup	lemon	butter
bread	carrot	flour	sandwich	mango	pasta	sausage	water
rice	milk	meat	coconut	grape	tea	pea	cheese
vegetable	picnic	olives	dinner	beans	coffee	sugar	salt

How much?

Only a little.

2 Read and match.

1 In some countries there isn't
2 They couldn't make any bread
3 He didn't have many eggs,
4 We didn't feel well
5 They had too many strawberries,
6 She didn't eat much at lunchtime

a because she felt sick.
b enough food for everyone to eat. ☐1
c because they didn't have enough flour.
d so they decided to give some to their friends.
e so he bought some more at the supermarket.
f because we ate too much ice cream at the party.

3 Read and choose the right words.

1 I feel sick because I ate **too many** / (**too much**) chocolate this morning.
2 I can't buy that because I don't have **enough** / **too many** money.
3 Are there **too many** / **too much** sandwiches?
4 There aren't **enough** / **too much** buses in my town.
5 I like going to the beach when there aren't **too much** / **too many** people.
6 There isn't **enough** / **too much** juice for everyone.

4 Write four sentences about your city or town in your notebook.

There are too many cars.
There aren't enough parks.

Language: countable and uncountable nouns

Do the online activities on **Practice Extra** as you complete this unit.

1 Complete the sentences.

> aren't   don't have   enough
> is   too many   too much

1   There   *aren't*   enough sandwiches for us.

2   There are _____ people on this bus.

3   Do you have _____ time to help me with the cake, Peter?

4   Oh, no! I _____ enough money!

5   There _____ enough milk for everyone.

6   I think we have _____ homework this weekend.

2 Complete the conversation.
Write a letter (A–F) for each answer.

A   OK. We won't have sausages. I know. Let's have some rice and chicken.

B   Let me see. No, I'm sorry. We don't have enough spaghetti.

C   That's a good idea. So, it's chicken, rice, and a salad.

D   Yes, we all like pizza, but there isn't enough flour or enough cheese.

E   I don't know. What would you like?

F   How about some sausages and a salad?

1   What are we going to have for lunch, Dad? [E]

2   Can we have spaghetti, please? It's my favorite. ☐

3   What about pizza then? Can you make us a pizza, please? ☐

4   OK, Dad, what ideas do you have? ☐

5   Um, no, thanks. I've had too many sausages this week. I had some on Monday and yesterday. ☐

6   That sounds better. Can we have a salad, too, please? ☐

3 Write about the picture.
Use "too much," "too many," "enough," and the words in the box.

> banana   cake   chair
> fork   pasta   plate   water

There are enough chairs.

_____

_____

_____

_____

4 What do you think? Answer the questions.

1   Do you eat enough fruit?

_____

2   Do you eat enough fish?

_____

3   Do you eat too much sugar?

_____

4   Do you eat too much candy?

_____

5   Do you eat too many fries?

_____

6   Do you drink enough water?

_____

Label the pictures.

> butter   chopsticks   cookie   jam   pan   popcorn   sauce   ~~snack~~

1

snack

2

3

4

5

6

7

8

 Write the words.

1 We put this on food to make it taste better. It can be hot or cold. ___sauce___

2 This is something we eat between meals. _____

3 These pieces of wood or plastic are used for eating. _____

4 This is made from fruit. We can put it on bread. _____

5 We use this to cook in. _____

6 A lot of children like this snack. It's often round. _____

7 This snack is popular when people go to the movies. _____

8 You can put this on the bread first when you make sandwiches. _____

 Write definitions for these words.

1 cereal _____

_____

2 strawberry _____

_____

3 sushi _____

_____

 Read and complete the sentences with 1, 2, 3, or 4 words.

Potato chips are very popular as a snack all over the world. George Crum invented them in the U.S.A. At the restaurant where he worked, fries were popular. One day someone wasn't happy because the fries were too thick. Crum made them thinner and thinner until finally, he made fries that were too thin to eat with a fork. The man in the restaurant was happy, and people around the world started to eat potato chips. In the U.K., chips are called "crisps," and fries are called "chips."

1 Potato chips are a ___very popular___ snack all over the world.

2 A man from _____ invented them.

3 He made the first chips because a man thought his fries _____.

4 Finally, Crum made fries that were _____ with a fork.

5 Chips are called "crisps" in the _____.

1 Match the children to their snacks. Write sentences.

Helen   Tanaz   Michael

Kito   Akash   Robert

1 Helen's favorite snack is bread and butter.
2 _____
3 _____
4 _____
5 _____
6 _____

2 Read the poem. Find the word.

The first letter in "snack." I'm hungry, you see. [s]

The second in "jam." The fruit's from a tree. [ ]

The third in "sausage." A hot dog to eat. [ ]

The fourth in "popcorn." Salted or sweet. [ ]

The fifth in "butter." I love it on bread. [ ]

It has something to do with food, I said.

Look at the word and write the letter.

With me, for sure, a dish will taste better.

What am I? _____

3 Read and answer "yes" or "no."

Chopsticks

People in Asia use many different things to eat with, for example, hands, spoons, forks, knives, and chopsticks.

Chopsticks can be big or small. Most Chinese chopsticks are about 25 cm long. For cooking, they also use longer chopsticks, which can be more than 50 cm long. In Japan, chopsticks are shorter, and they come to a point at one end.

Chopsticks are made of a number of materials, but most are made of wood or plastic. A long time ago, they put silver on the end of the chopsticks.

Things you should or shouldn't do when you eat with chopsticks

- Do not move your chopsticks around.
- Do not pick food up by making a hole in it with your chopsticks.
- Do not pull dishes toward you with chopsticks. Use your hands.
- Pull dishes close to you when eating. Put them back after you use them.
- You can lift your dish up to your mouth to eat small pieces of food.

1 Chopsticks are always 25 cm long.
   no
2 They are the same size in Japan and China. _____
3 They are usually made of plastic or wood. _____
4 You should use them to make holes. _____
5 You should use them to pull dishes toward you. _____
6 You should use them to pick up pieces of your food. _____

Sounds and life skills
Exploring food from other cultures
Pronunciation focus

 1 🎧 14 **Listen and circle the strong words.**

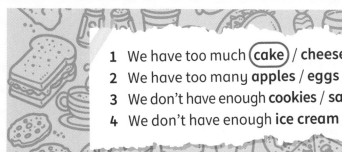

1 We have too much (cake) / cheese / sugar!
2 We have too many **apples** / eggs / sausages!
3 We don't have enough **cookies** / sandwiches / watermelon!
4 We don't have enough **ice cream** / water / lemonade!

 2 🎧 15 **Read and complete with your own words. Listen and say.**

We're having a picnic, but we have too many _____ and too much _____ ,
but we don't have any _____ ! What are we going to do?

 3 **Read and complete.**

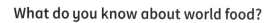
apples   bread   Empanadas   India   ~~rice~~   Sashimi

What do you know about world food?

1 You will find a lot of _____*rice*_____ in Spanish paella.

2 Tandoori chicken comes from _____ .

3 _____ is made of raw fish and comes from Japan.

4 _____ are delicious pastries, usually with meat inside.

5 You need _____ to make tarte Tatin.

6 Simit is a Turkish _____ in the shape of a circle.

4 **Complete with your ideas.**

My favorite food is _____ .
I like food from _____ .
I've never eaten _____ .
Today, I've eaten _____ .
I sometimes eat too many _____ .
I don't eat enough _____ .

Read and answer.

1 Why will Diggory have to work quickly? They only have enough food for three days.
2 When will Iyam tell Diggory where the Sun Stone is? _____
3 Where are the secret caves? _____
4 Why was corn important to the Mayas and the Aztecs? _____
5 What did the Aztecs put in their chocolate? _____
6 What else did the Aztecs eat? _____

 Correct the sentences.

1 Emily didn't ask Iyam enough questions.
   Emily asked Iyam too many questions.
2 There are pictures of sushi on the Sun Stone.

3 Butter was the most important Aztec food.

4 The door to the caves is about three kilometers west.

5 Iyam shouldn't run because the ground is moving.

6 Diggory asked Emily to get him some chopsticks.

Do you remember?

1 We have too ___many___ strawberries.
2 We don't have _____ milk.
3 I love butter and strawberry _____ on my bread in the morning.
4 People in China often use _____ to eat with.
5 _____ is a Spanish rice dish.
6 We cook _____ in a pan of boiling water.

Can do

I can use countable and uncountable nouns.

I can talk about food.

I can write about my favorite food.

How does food get to your table?

1 **Read and complete with the correct form of the verbs.**

~~grow~~   make   plant   prepare   take   wash

Potatoes: from field to fork

1 Potatoes _____grow_____ from spring to fall.

2 First, a large machine _____ the fields for potato planting.

3 Then farmers _____ potato seeds about 15 cm underground.

4 A large machine collects the potatoes when they're ready. Next, trucks _____ the potatoes to a factory.

5 After that, factory workers _____ and then sort the potatoes into different sizes.

6 Finally, we can eat the potatoes! We often _____ them into fries and chips.

 2 **Plan to write an article. Complete the table about a food or drink.**

What is the food or drink?	
Where/When does it grow?	It grows / They grow in/on _____ .
When is the harvest?	
How does it get to your table?	First, _____ . Then _____ . Next, _____ . After that, _____ . Finally, _____ .
How can people eat or drink it?	

 3 📝 **Use your notes to write your article.**

4 **Did you ...**
- ☐ plan your article?
- ☐ use sequencing words?
- ☐ use the correct words to show each step of the process?
- ☐ read your article again?
- ☐ check grammar, spelling, and punctuation?

Writing tip

Writing an article
Use sequencing words like *first*, *then*, *next*, *after that*, and *finally* to make your article easy for other people to understand.

Flyers Reading and Writing

1 Look at the three pictures. Write about this story. Write 20 or more words.

1 **Read the story. Choose a word from the box. Write the correct word next to numbers 1–8.**

backpack   camp   campsite   chopsticks   ~~country~~   enough   flashlight
hungry   map   pasta   sandwiches   tents   too   was   were

FRIENDLY

Last week's episode of *Friendly* was really funny because there was a field trip to the _____country_____ . The teachers were taking their students to a forest to (1) _____ . On Friday afternoon, when they were waiting for the bus outside the school, Jenny arrived with a really big heavy suitcase. She said that her (2) _____ wasn't very big, and she had a lot of equipment.

On the way to the campsite, Sally sat next to the bus driver because she wanted to watch her drive, look at the directions, and follow them on her (3) _____ .

When they got to the forest, all five of them had to help Jenny pull her suitcase across the field to the (4) _____ . The ground was too soft, and it was really hard work. When they were pulling the suitcase, it fell down again and again.

It was dinnertime when they arrived at the campsite, and they were dirty, tired, and (5) _____ . Jenny wasn't very happy when she discovered she couldn't use her hairdryer. She was surprised because she couldn't connect it to any electricity in the wall of the tent! Peter was really unhappy because he wanted to cook sausages and beans, but Jim thought a fire was (6) _____ dangerous in a forest. Jim took some peanut butter and jam (7) _____ out of his backpack, Sally said she had some popcorn and cookies, and they all laughed when Frankie said she was carrying enough cold sushi and (8) _____ for everyone!
They all agreed that they were eating the strangest camp menu ever!

2 **Choose a title for this episode of *Friendly*.**

Mark (✓) one box.   A drive in the country ☐   An unusual dinner ☐   Forest fire ☐

3 **Which one is not like the others and why?**

1 soup   butter   jam   (cookie)
It's countable. _____

2 chopsticks   fork   flashlight   spoon
_____

3 best   north   east   south
_____

4 sandwich   sauce   pan   snack
_____

5 tent   cave   sleeping bag   backpack
_____

6 pasta   bread   cake   cheese
_____

4 Complete the sentences. Count and write the letters.

1 The opposite of "east" is _____west_____ . [4]

2 Another word for a long trip is _____ . ☐

3 A _____ is like a small house. We sleep in it when we camp. ☐

4 A _____ is higher than a hill. ☐

5 They use _____ to eat sushi in Japan. ☐

6 We use a _____ to see in the dark when we go camping. ☐

7 I don't like this soup. There's _____ much salt in it. ☐

8 Go from one place to another. _____ ☐

9 How _____ butter do we need? ☐

10 A bag that we carry on our back is a _____ . ☐

11 There were too _____ people at the beach. ☐

12 "What _____ he doing when he fell?" "He was skiing." ☐

13 Something light that we eat between meals when we're hungry is a _____ . ☐

14 We only had 50 g of flour. It wasn't _____ flour to make cookies. ☐

5 Now complete the crossword. Write the message.

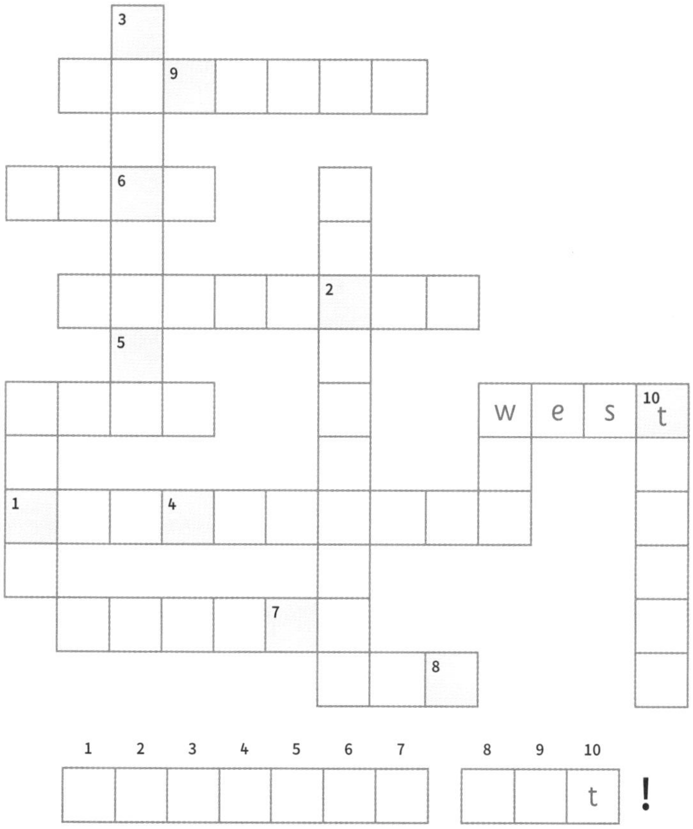

(crossword grid with numbered squares 1–10; filled letters: w e s t at row marked 10, "t" in numbered cells)

1 2 3 4 5 6 7   8 9 10

_ _ _ _ _ _ _   _ _ t !

6 Quiz time!

1 When did Robert break his arm?
When he was _____

2 What pushes together to make a mountain range? _____

3 What's the world's oldest mountain range? _____

4 Why couldn't Sally, Robert, and Eva make the cake? _____

5 What climate do apples need to grow? _____

6 How many different types of apples are there around the world? _____

7 📝 Write questions for your quiz in your notebook.

5 Under the ocean

We **still** haven't chosen a project. (= But we have to do it soon.)

The rescue team has been here **since** ten o'clock. (= When? A point in time: time, date, day, etc.)

It's been here **for** about three hours. (= How long? How many minutes, hours, days, weeks, etc.)

 1 Read and choose the right words.

1 Mr. Schwarz has taught me German (for) / since / still three years.

2 It hasn't snowed since **three days / Saturday / two weeks.**

3 I **still / for / since** haven't finished this activity.

4 They **are / have / were** worked here for a year.

5 She hasn't caught a fish **for / since / still** two hours.

 2 Complete the sentences with "for" or "since."

1 She's lived in her town _____since_____ 2008.

2 My little brother has studied English _____ six months.

3 I haven't seen Deniz _____ Monday.

4 Mom's had her favorite jacket _____ ten years!

5 I haven't eaten anything _____ nine o'clock.

 3 Look at the code (a = ____). Write the secret message.

a	b	c
d	e	f
g	h	i

j	k	l
m	n	o
p	q	r

s	t	u
v	w	x
y	z	

I ' v e

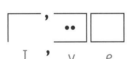

4 📝 Write a message in code in your notebook.

📱 Do the online activities on **Practice Extra** as you complete this unit.

Find and write four sentences.

liked fishing	three o'clock.	this class since
in that house for	five years.	We've been in
~~He's loved~~	I've	for nine months.
started school.	They've lived	~~math since he~~

He's loved math since he _____

_____

 Write sentences about you with "for" or "since."

1 (this room)   I've been in this room for ten minutes.
2 (this class) _____
3 (best friend) _____
4 (this school) _____
5 (my house)   _____
6 (English)   _____

 Use the ideas in Activity 2 to write questions to ask your partner.

1 How long have you been in this room?
2 _____
3 _____
4 _____
5 _____
6 _____

 Read and complete the table.

It's 12 o'clock. There are four children on a bus. Peter was the first boy on the bus. He's been on the bus for ten minutes now, but he's going to get off at the next stop, in two minutes.
David was the last to get on. He got on two minutes ago, but he's going to get off last.
Anika has been on the bus for four minutes. She's going to get off at the same stop as Emma.
Emma has been on the bus for the same time as Anika. She's going to get off at the stop after Peter, in four minutes.
Anika and Emma are going to get off the bus seven minutes before David.

	Got on the bus?	Going to get off the bus?	How long on the bus in total?
Peter	11:50		
David			
Anika			
Emma			

Look and complete the crossword.

| ¹j | e | l | ²l | y | f | i | ³s | h |

4 | 5

6 | | | | | | | 7

 Write the words.

1 Big ones have the biggest eyes in the world. _____squid_____

2 It has eight legs, but it doesn't have a shell. _____

3 It has no brain or bones, but it eats tiny fish and animals. _____

4 The salt water that covers Earth. _____

5 It has eight legs, two claws, and a hard shell. It walks from side to side. _____

6 It's a mammal that lives in the ocean. It isn't a dolphin or a whale. _____

7 It's an ocean animal that forms reefs. _____

8 It's an ocean animal with big claws and a hard shell. _____

 Read, look, and write the words.

(1) _____Fishing_____ is a very important activity. Every year people eat more than 100 million

metric tons of (2) _____ (one metric ton is a thousand kilos). That's a lot of fish, so we need to

be careful and not catch too many.

People don't only eat fish, though. In different countries, people eat a lot of other ocean animals.

Inuit people eat (3) _____ . In Japan and Greece, (4) _____ and

(5) _____ are favorite foods, and (6) _____ are popular all over the world.

In some countries, for example, the U.S.A. and France, people pay a lot of (7) _____ to eat

(8) _____ .

1 Circle 12 words. Which two are different? Why?

beautiful (loud) angerous strong great urtle xcited dolphin icexciting good irty

_____ and _____ are different. They are _____ .

2 Compare these ocean animals. Use adjectives from Activity 1 and your own ideas.

1 jellyfish – seals Jellyfish are more dangerous than seals.
2 coral – an octopus
3 an octopus – a jellyfish
4 turtles – lobsters
5 a whale – a squid
6 a shark – a crab

3 Read and color and write.

Find the octopus that is sitting on the big rock and color it purple. Next, find the squid (there are three) and color the smallest one yellow. At the bottom of the picture, there's a lot of coral. Color it red. Have you found the lobster? It's in the bottom right corner. Write "lobster" above it. At the top of the picture, there are some jellyfish. Color the biggest one blue. Finally, there's only one more animal to color. Find the crab (there are three) inside the shell. Color it pink.

4 Read and match.

1 The world's first coral reef	a is the Great Barrier Reef in Australia.
2 Storms can	b appeared about 500 million years ago. [1]
3 Scientists have used coral reefs	c they make beautiful white sand.
4 When parrot fish eat coral,	d to make a lot of different medicines.
5 The biggest reef in the world	e break coral reefs.

Sounds and life skills
Finding out more
Pronunciation focus

 16 **Listen and circle the correct word.**

1 The (people) / team pulled the **dolphin / boat** back to the **beach / park**.

2 My **mother / sister** and **father / brother** like to eat **breakfast / dinner** together.

3 A **dolphin / penguin** can swim in different kinds of **water / weather**.

4 Look over **here / there**! My brother's bought a **blue / purple** and red **bike / parrot**.

 17 **Complete with the words from Activity 1. Listen and check.**

/p/	/b/	/d/	/ ð/
			mother

 Read and write the questions.

a / fire? / there / Is

A: What's happening? (1) *Is there a fire?*

B: No, the firefighters are rescuing a cat.

the / now? / cat / right / Where's

A: (2) _____

B: Look! It's up there in that tree.

time? / Has / been / there / a / it / long

A: (3) _____

B: It's been there since eight o'clock this morning.

firefighters / What / the / done? / have

A: (4) _____

B: They've put up a ladder.

they / to / do? / going / What / are

A: (5) _____

B: They are going to climb the ladder and bring the cat down.

 Read and complete. arrived   called   climbed   had   ~~rescued~~   is   was

This afternoon, firefighters (1) ___ rescued ___ Tilly the cat from a very tall tree on Pine Grove Road. Tilly (2) _____ in the tree for a long time. The family (3) _____ the firefighters, and they (4) _____ at 12 o'clock. They put up a ladder and (5) _____ the tree. Tilly the cat (6) _____ now safe at home with her family. What an adventure she's (7) _____ !

1 **Read and answer.**

1 What has Emily found? She's found a flashlight.
2 What did Quetzalcóatl get at Teotihuacán?
3 What kind of shell has Diggory seen?
4 Why's Iyam like this animal?
5 Was gold a treasure for the Aztecs?
6 What's Richard going to do if they don't help Iyam?

2 **Write sentences from the story.**

1 You / pull / these plants / you / open / this cave
You've pulled these plants, and you've opened this cave.
2 I / find / flashlight

3 I / know / about / these caves / 1971

4 This / be / place / their gods / make / sun / moon / universe

5 There / be / gold here / hundreds of years

6 Richard / use / my cell phone / follow us

Do you remember?

1 I've been here _____since_____ seven o'clock.
2 She's lived in this town _____ five years.
3 _____ have been in our oceans for 650 million years.
4 I think _____ reefs are really beautiful.
5 Giant squids have the _____ eyes in the world.
6 Seals have swum in our oceans for 22 million _____ .

Can do

I can talk about things that have happened using *for* and *since*.

I can talk about ocean animals.

I can write about ocean animals.

How can we make electricity?

1 Read and complete.

> Another reason is that   Firstly, it's a   On the other hand, a disadvantage of
> ~~There are a lot of advantages to~~   To sum up, I think that

Study Guide Page 12

Geothermal energy

Inside our planet, it's very hot. Geothermal energy uses the heat from the Earth to make electricity. The heat is under the ground, and special buildings called power plants change the heat into electricity. (1) _There are a lot of advantages to_ geothermal energy. (2) _____ renewable source of energy, and it doesn't pollute the environment. (3) _____ it's a good way to create electricity in areas where there are volcanoes, like in Iceland. (4) _____ geothermal energy is that the power plants are very expensive to build. (5) _____ geothermal energy, like solar, wind, and wave energy, is a really good source of renewable energy.

2 Plan to write an essay. Complete the table on a source of renewable energy.

Introduction	_____ is a type of renewable energy, which means it uses _____ .
Advantages	There are a lot of reasons why people think _____ is a good idea. Firstly, _____ . Another reason is that _____ . Finally, _____ .
Disadvantages	On the other hand, a disadvantage of _____ is that _____ .
Ending	To sum up, I believe that _____ .

3 Use your notes to write your essay.

4 Did you ...

- ☐ plan your essay?
- ☐ include an introduction and an ending?
- ☐ use topic sentences?
- ☐ read your essay again?
- ☐ check grammar, spelling, and punctuation?

Writing tip

Writing an essay

You can organize the information in your essay with an **introduction**, some **advantages**, some **disadvantages**, and an **ending**. Topic sentences help you introduce a new idea in each part of your essay.

Flyers Reading and Writing

1 **Sarah is talking to her friend. What does Katy say to Sarah?**

Read the conversation and choose the best answer.
Write a letter (A–E) for each answer.
There is one example.

Example

Sarah: Hi, Katy! I haven't seen you for a long time.
Katy: C

Questions

1   Sarah: That's nice. Did you go anywhere interesting?
       Katy: _____

2   Sarah: Oh! I haven't been there. Did you like it?
       Katy: _____

3   Sarah: I'll ask my mom to take me next week.
       Katy: _____

4   Sarah: Which day is the best to go, do you think?
       Katy: _____

A   Yes, it was great. There were a lot of things to do.

B   Friday. That's when you can swim with the dolphins.

C   I know. I've been on vacation. **(Example)**

D   Yes. I went to the Ocean Life Center.

E   That's a good idea.

Free time

some	any	no	every
someone	**any**one	**no** one	**every**one
something	**any**thing	**no**thing	**every**thing
somewhere	**any**where	**no**where	**every**where

1 **Read the test carefully. Follow the instructions.**

Reading Test	

1 First read ALL of the instructions.

2 Write the name of someone you like.

_____

3 Think of somewhere you like to go.

_____

4 Name something you can use to write with.

_____

5 Write your full name.

_____

6 Write somewhere you can sleep.

_____

7 Only write the answers to numbers 5 and 8.

_____

8 Name someone who teaches you.

_____

2 **Read and choose the right words.**

1 I can't see (**anything**) / **something**.

2 Is there **everywhere** / **anywhere** I can sit down?

3 I couldn't find my book, and I looked **everywhere** / **somewhere**.

4 Can **no one** / **anyone** give me a pencil, please?

5 Do you have **nothing** / **anything** made of plastic?

6 **Everyone** / **Anyone** stand up, please.

3 **Read and complete.**

> anyone   everywhere
> everywhere   inside
> ~~no one~~   no one

A man is watching TV when he hears the doorbell. He opens the door, but (1) ___no one___ is there. He looks (2) _____ :

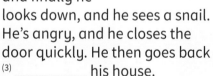

to the left, to the right, up, and finally he looks down, and he sees a snail. He's angry, and he closes the door quickly. He then goes back (3) _____ his house.

A month later, the same thing happens. He opens the door, but there isn't (4) _____ there. He looks (5) _____ , but there's (6) _____ there. Finally, he looks down and sees the snail again. Before he can close the door quickly again, the snail asks, "Why did you do that?"

4 **Tell the story in the past. Write it in your notebook.**

☐ Do the online activities on **Practice Extra** as you complete this unit.

1 Read and answer.

1 In this sport, everyone wears cleats. There are 11 players on a team, and anyone can kick something that is round. Not everyone can catch the round thing. Only one player can do that.

  a What's the thing that they kick?
      a ball

  b What's the sport? _____

  c Who are the people who play this sport?

2 In this sport, someone puts some long things on their feet and goes to the top of a hill or a mountain. They go down the hill over something that is cold and white.

  a What are the long things that they put on their feet? _____

  b What are they doing? _____

  c What's the thing that is cold and white? _____

3 In this sport, everyone uses something long to hit something that is very small and round. No one can kick, catch, or throw the small round thing. They have to hit it into a small hole.

  a What's the sport? _____

  b Do you play it inside or outside? _____

  c Where is the hole? _____

 2 **Write a definition for a sport or a hobby. Use the words from the "Study again" box on page 54.**

_____

_____

_____

_____

 3 Match the sentences to the pictures.

  a Would anyone like to play tennis?
  b Let's go somewhere different on vacation this year.
  c No one wants to play soccer today.
  d There's nowhere for us to play.

4 Read and order the text.

☐ but No One did it. Someone was angry, because it really was something that Everyone

☐ In the end, Everyone was really angry with Someone when No One did what Anyone could do.

[1] Once upon a time, there were four children in a class. Their names

☐ classroom. Everyone thought that Someone was going to do it. It wasn't difficult, so Anyone could do it,

☐ could do. Everyone thought that Anyone could do it, but No One thought that Everyone wasn't going to do it.

☐ were No One, Anyone, Someone, and Everyone. Their teacher asked for some help in the

1 Label the pictures.

1 b e a t b o x   3 _____   5 _____

2 _____   4 _____

2 Follow the free-time words.

hobby	does	ballet dancing	sewing	playing the piano	baseball
fashion design	to	beatbox	Someone	different	chess
skateboarding	places	Ping-Pong	bored.	goes	skating
mountain biking	things	cooking	interesting	never	reading
board games	skiing	golf	and	is	who

3 Look at the other words in Activity 2. Use them to write a sentence.

Someone _____

_____

4 Read and answer.

When people first started free running, they did it to get from one place to another using the quickest path. They ran and jumped from wall to wall and down steps. Now they try to do it in the most beautiful way possible. Free running is similar to Parkour.

In Britain, free running became popular in 2003 after someone made a TV show about it.

Free running has also been in music videos by pop stars, and we can see it in action movies and commercials on TV. There is also a video game called *Free Running*.

It is important to remember that it is something that not everyone can do because free runners need to be really strong and in very good shape. It is also difficult, and it can be dangerous.

1 What do free runners do? They run and jump from wall to wall and down steps.

2 When did free running become popular in Britain? _____

3 Where can you see free running? _____

4 Can everyone do free running? _____

5 Why / Why not? _____

1 Find and say four differences. Then write sentences.

In picture "a," a girl and a boy are playing chess. In picture "b," two girls are playing.

 2 Read the email. Choose the right words and write them on the lines.

Hi Betty,
How are you? Did (1)___you___ have a good vacation? (2)_____ was great. I went to a special activity camp, and I've started some new hobbies. (3)_____ was at the camp for five days, and (4)_____ did something different every day! The first two days it was raining, so we did puzzles and played board games, and I learned to play chess. I also designed some clothes!
On Wednesday, they took (5)_____ to the hills where we rode amazing mountain bikes. It was really exciting. William taught (6)_____ how to skateboard on Thursday morning, so I spent all afternoon skateboarding with my friends. Friday was (7)_____ last day, and we did beatbox and rap!
(8)_____ only problem now is that I have too many hobbies!
Holly

1	they	you	us
2	Mine	I	You
3	He	We	I
4	him	we	them
5	we	they	us
6	me	her	you
7	his	me	our
8	I	Me	My

 3 Write questions for the answers.

1 Where did she go?
She went to an activity camp.

2 _____
She was there for five days.

3 _____
Because it was raining.

4 _____
She learned to play chess.

5 _____
They rode amazing mountain bikes.

6 _____
They did beatbox and rap.

 4 In your notebook, write an email to a friend about your hobbies.

Vocabulary: hobbies   57

Sounds and life skills
Imagining and inventing

Pronunciation focus

1 🎧 18 **Listen and draw arrows ↗.**

Joe: I'm bored! Dad, can I use yesterday's newspaper, please? ↗

Dad: Yes, of course.

Hannah: Mom, can I have that old flowerpot, please?

Mom: Yes. Here you are.

2 📝 **Write questions asking a friend for different things. Then draw arrows ↗.**

Ebony, can I borrow your bike tomorrow, please? ↗

1 _____

2 _____

3 _____

3 **Read and complete. Then look and match.** boots bottles paper shells ~~sock~~

 1 | c
 2 |
 3 |
 4 |
 5 |

a Collect _____ on the beach and make this wind instrument.

b Paint old glass and plastic _____ and make a chess game!

c You can use a ___sock___ to make a puppet.

d Recycle _____ and make planes for a flying competition.

e Use these _____ for your plants!

4 📝 **Explain how you can reuse an object. Draw a picture to help you.**

Use a _____

_____

_____

_____

_____

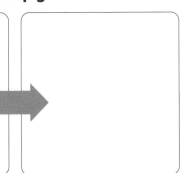

1 Read and answer.

Diggory Bones

1 Where are they going to go? Somewhere closer to the ocean.
2 What will take Iyam to a cave of gold? _____
3 Are Kukulcán and Quetzalcóatl the same? _____

_____

4 What's Kukulcán's temple called? _____

_____

5 What did the Mayas do before their ball game? _____

_____

6 In which months can you see the snake on the stairs? _____

A Mayan ball court

2 Look at the code. Write the secret message in your notebook.

| N = north |
| E = east |
| S = south |
| W = west |

Tlachtli – 5E – 4S – 2W – 3N – 3W – 3S – 4E – 4N – 1S – 3W – 3S – 2N – 4E – 2W –
2N – 1W – 4S – 1N – 2W – 5E – 2N – 3W – 1S – 2W – 4E – 1S – 1W – 2W – 3N.

Tlachtli	walls.	ball	rubber	played.	was
that	had	stone	game	They	of
up	pass	high	heavy	on	a
circle	the	a	of	one	made
Mayan	to	through	ball	men	a

Do you remember?

1 Is there _____anywhere_____ I can sit down?
2 I've looked _____ , but I can't find my pen.
3 _____ is a very old board game.
4 Music and rhythm that you make with your mouth is called _____ .
5 I enjoy riding on the bike _____ in the mountains.
6 My friend has (play) _____ soccer for six years.

Can do

I can use *something*, *anything*, *nothing*, and *everything*.

I can talk about different hobbies.

I can write about sports and activities.

What makes an amusement park ride exciting and safe?

 1 **Read and complete.**

different   fantastic   ~~new~~   scarier   strange   under

A day at the amusement park

Last weekend, I went to an amusement park with my friends because we wanted to try a **(1)** _new_ rollercoaster called Upside Down.

It was **(2)** _____ from all of the other rollercoasters that I've been on because, on this rollercoaster, you ride **(3)** _____ the tracks! We sat in seats with our legs hanging free, which felt very **(4)** _____ at first. Of course we wore a harness, too.

I thought the ride was **(5)** _____ than other rollercoasters because there were twists and turns and we went around five different loops. It was **(6)** _____! I want to go back to the amusement park again soon just to ride on Upside Down.

2 **Plan to write a story about an amusement park ride. Complete the table.**

Paragraph 1	When was it? Where were you? Who were you with?	
Paragraph 2	What happened? How did you feel?	
Paragraph 3	What happened in the end? How did you feel?	

 3 **Use your notes to write your story.**

 4 **Did you ...**
- ☐ plan your story?
- ☐ include a beginning, middle, and ending?
- ☐ use interesting adjectives to tell your story?
- ☐ read your story again?
- ☐ check grammar, spelling, and punctuation?

Writing tip

Writing a story

When you write a story about something that has already happened, you can use **past verbs** and a lot of different **adjectives** to make your story interesting.

I **went** to a big amusement park with my friends last week. It **was** really **exciting** because …

Flyers Reading and Writing

1 **Read the story. Choose a word from the box. Write the correct word next to numbers 1–5. There is one example.**

example				
help	them	playing	basement	space
often	plays	want	parents	country

Rachel and Paul ___help___ at an animal rescue center in their free time. They **(1)** _____ go there on weekends. They love **(2)** _____ with the dogs and cats. They also help take care of **(3)** _____ . They feed the animals and clean their boxes. They really enjoy doing this because they love animals.

They sometimes go to a special market with their **(4)** _____ and other grown-ups. At the market, they sell things to get money for the rescue center. They also ask other people to help them. One day, a rich and famous actor went to the rescue center and took two big dogs and three cats home to his house in the **(5)** _____ . He lives in a castle!

(6) **Now choose the best name for the story.**

Mark (✓) one box.

Friends and family ☐

Pet rescue ☐

A day at the market ☐

Review Units 5 and 6

1 **Read the story. Choose a word from the box. Write the correct word next to numbers 1–8.**

> anything   chess   cook   coral reef   dangerous   everyone   ~~hobbies~~
> no one   nowhere   ocean   ridden   safe   someone   squid   vacation

FRIENDLY

In today's episode, the friends are talking about the ___hobbies___ that they do in their free time. Jim's started free running and is really excited about it. He says he got the idea when he saw the movie *Captain America: The Winter Soldier* and the hero had to run through a city's downtown. Sally says she loves action movies and that there are special actors who do all the tricks. Her favorite is Maxine Limit. Maxine has driven cars at over 200 kilometers an hour, she's flown a lot of different planes, and she's (1) _____ motorcycles, horses, and elephants. Jenny doesn't find any of this exciting, and she tells Jim that she thinks his new hobby is strange and too (2) _____ .

Frankie's hobby isn't dangerous, but once, when she was painting a small waterfall in the country, she fell into the river, which was moving very fast, and (3) _____ had to pull her out. Peter loves trying new things to eat. He says he'll try anything. He's eaten octopus and (4) _____ before, but on his last (5) _____ in Japan, he and his parents ate blowfish. This fish is very, very poisonous, and someone has to prepare and (6) _____ it really well, or you can die when you eat it. Jenny tries to remember the most dangerous thing she's ever done. Jim laughs because he can't believe she's ever done (7) _____ dangerous. Jenny says that once she ate one of Frankie's dishes, and (8) _____ knows that she's a terrible cook!

2 **Choose a title for this episode of *Friendly*.**

Mark (✓) one box.   Living dangerously ☐   Hard actors ☐   Eating seafood ☐

3 **Which is not like the others and why?**

1 golf (badminton) soccer tennis
   You don't play it with a ball.

2 seen ridden walked thought

3 baseball volleyball soccer basketball

4 crab jellyfish lobster turtle

5 skates skis chess skateboards

6 octopus jellyfish seal clownfish

4 Complete the sentences. Count and write the letters.

1 "How many fish has that dolphin ___eaten___?" "Six." `5`

2 In _____ people run and jump in a city's downtown. ☐

3 An ocean animal without claws that has eight legs. It isn't a squid.
_____ ☐

4 _____ is a black and white board game. ☐

5 An _____ is usually bigger than seas, rivers, and lakes. ☐

6 "Is there _____ in the café?" "No, everyone's gone." ☐

7 A _____ is something hard on the outside of an animal's body. A turtle has one. ☐

8 We stand on a _____ to go fast in parks. ☐

9 A _____ is a round animal with eight legs and two arms with claws. ☐

10 He's been a soccer player _____ 2005. ☐

11 _____ looks like a little forest, but it's a lot of ocean animals. ☐

12 A _____ is in the same family as dolphins and seals, but it's much bigger. ☐

13 A bat is _____ that we use to hit a ball. ☐

14 "How long have you _____ your mountain bike?" "For a year." ☐

15 He's been a photographer _____ nine years. ☐

5 Now complete the crossword. Write the message.

e a t e ⁸n

| 1 | 2 | 3 | 3 | | 4 | 5 | 6 | 3 | | 1 | 7 | 8 |

☐☐☐☐☐ - ☐☐☐☐☐   ☐☐ n !

6 Quiz time!

1 What were the people rescuing on the beach? A dolphin.

2 Where does solar energy come from?

3 Where does hydro energy come from?

4 What do Robert, Sally, and Eva play in the classroom?

5 Do rollercoasters have engines?

7 Write questions for your quiz in your notebook.

7 Fashion sense

I think it **may look** better with a jacket.	I **might buy** a new jacket.
I **might not need** a jacket.	She **may go** to the party.

1 **Circle 12 words. Which two are different? Why?**

jeansneakershoeskirtshirtennishortsocksweaterunninglassescarf

_____ and _____ are different.

They are _____ .

2 **Read and choose the right words.**

1 He (**may buy**) / **may buys** / **may to buy** some new sneakers.

2 She **mights wear** / **might wears** / **might wear** her gold bracelet.

3 It **not might** / **might not** / **isn't might** be cold.

4 You **may want** / **mays want** / **may wants** olives on your pizza.

5 They **can't might** / **might not** / **don't might** win this afternoon's game.

6 You **might** / **can't** / **can** need a scarf because I think it's cold outside!

3 **Write about your clothes.**

1 My sneakers are made of _____ .

2 My jacket is made of _____ .

3 My shoes _____ .

4 Tomorrow I might wear _____ because _____ .

5 On the weekend, I might wear _____ because _____ .

4 **Complete the sentences.** ⟨ get   get up   go   visit   watch   ~~wear~~ ⟩

1 He might _____wear_____ a jacket this afternoon because it's cold.

2 She might _____ TV after lunch.

3 They might _____ us today.

4 You might not _____ your present until Sunday.

5 I may not _____ shopping tomorrow.

6 We may _____ early on Saturday.

▶ Do the online activities on **Practice Extra** as you complete this unit.

What do you think it is? Use "may."

It may be _____ _____ _____ _____

 Look at the picture. Read and answer "yes" or "no."

1 They might have a picnic.   *yes*
2 She might be lost. _____
3 He may want to catch a bus home. _____
4 She might not be happy. _____
5 It might rain. _____
6 They might need coats. _____

 Correct the sentences.

1 They mights wear their jeans. They might wear their jeans.
2 She does might take a jacket. _____
3 I don't might put on my sweater. _____
4 Lucas may plays soccer tomorrow. _____
5 I might not to wear my black shoes. _____
6 They mays wear their new sneakers. _____

4 📝 **Find and write five sentences.**

Susan	might put	is green	coats and scarves.
Our school	took	of	and red.
Kito	uniform	on their	plastic.
My schoolbag's	wore her	blue polka-dot	with him.
The children	made	a jacket	belt.

1 Susan wore her blue polka-dot belt.
2 _____
3 _____
4 _____
5 _____

Find two words for each group of letters. One is a clothes word.

1 tr- _____tree_____ , _____traffic_____
2 sh- _____ , _____
3 po- _____ , _____
4 gl- _____ , _____
5 u- _____ , _____
6 bu- _____ , _____

mbrella   oves   ee   ue   orts   affic   gly   tter   oes   cket   tato   tton

 Label the pictures with clothes words from Activity 1.

1 2 3 4 5 6

pocket

 Read and complete the sentences with 1, 2, 3, or 4 words.

Last Saturday, Oliver went shopping with his uncle Harry to buy some new clothes. They went to three different clothing stores. The first store was called Legs Eleven, and they had a lot of socks. Oliver chose some gray and green ones.

Next they went to look for some shorts. They found a lot in a store called 4 Fashion. Oliver didn't know which ones to choose, so his uncle helped him. He got a cool orange pair made of cotton with big pockets.

In the last store, they bought a striped brown and red coat. He didn't buy any new sneakers because he has three pairs at home. When they were coming home, it started to rain, so they bought two umbrellas from a small store. They caught the bus home because they didn't want to get wet.

1 Oliver went to the stores with _____his uncle Harry_____ .
2 Legs Eleven was _____ store that they went into.
3 Oliver's new socks are _____ .
4 Uncle Harry helped Oliver _____ some shorts.
5 Oliver's new orange shorts are made of _____ , and they have big pockets.
6 He didn't need _____ because he has three pairs.
7 They got a striped _____ in the last clothing store.
8 They went home on _____ because it was raining.

Vocabulary: fashion and adjectives

1 **Read and complete the circle with names and clothes words.**

Three girls and two boys are sitting around a table. Frank is sitting between two girls. The girl on his left is named Emma.

The girl on William's left is named Betty.

The girl between Frank and Sarah is wearing a striped T-shirt and a skirt. She has a beautiful gold ring.

The boy with the shorts is wearing a belt. He's also wearing a shirt and a new jacket.

The girl with the scarf isn't wearing a skirt. She's wearing some pants and a sweater that is made of cotton.

The girl on the right of Frank has some plastic earrings on. She's also wearing a striped sweater, a skirt, and sneakers.

The other boy is cold, so he's wearing some gloves. His sweater is striped, and he's also wearing pants.

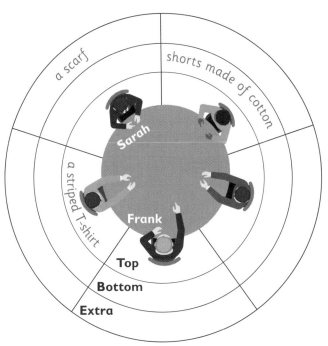

2 **Draw a piece of clothing and write about it in your notebook.**

These are my favorite shorts. They're very, very big, so I wear them with a belt. They're dark brown, and they have big pockets on the legs above the knees. My mom hates them, but I love them!

3 **Describe the picture.**

1 No one _____ is playing chess _____ .

2 Nothing _____
_____ .

3 No one _____
_____ .

4 Everyone _____
_____ .

5 Someone _____
_____ .

Sounds and life skills

Planning together

Pronunciation focus

1 🎧 19 **Circle the connected words. Listen and check. Then say.**

1 (That's a) (good idea)!

2 Let's decide on the music.

3 That jacket is great!

4 Come on, hurry up.

5 Look at all the balloons.

2 🎧 20 **Listen and write. Then circle the connected letters.**

1 Let's ____ pla(n o)ur ____ dance! | Can we ____ it ____ ?

2 We need to ____ on ____ day. | I think Friday ____ is the best.

3 How ____ a big pizza? | I ____ Italian food!

4 Let's ____ up a ____ of balloons! | We have a ____ of ideas!

3 🎧 21 **Listen and circle the correct information.**

1 **a** dance   **(b** party**)**   5 **a** green costumes   **b** silver costumes

2 **a** June   **b** September   6 **a** rock music   **b** electronic music

3 **a** 6:30   **b** 7:30   7 **a** star cakes   **b** moon cookies

4 **a** space   **b** aliens   8 **a** playground   **b** sports center

4 **Complete with words from Activity 3.**

We're having a ___party___ on Friday
____ 22nd at ____ in the evening.
The theme is ____, so please wear gold
or ____ .
There will be ____ and ____ !
It's going to be **OUT OF THIS WORLD** and out in the ____ !

   Sounds and life skills: connected speech | 🛡 collaboration

7

1 Read and answer.

Diggory Bones

1 What did Aztec braves wear? They wore birds' feathers and animal fur.
2 How did everyone feel when they saw them? _____
3 What did the Mayas do in the round building? _____
4 Why do they have to move fast? _____
5 When do the bowls work like mirrors? _____
6 At what time is the sun at its highest? _____

2 Put the verbs into the simple past.

The Aztecs (1) __were__ (are) very rich. They (2) _____ (have) fields and water to grow plants for food and materials. They also (3) _____ (have) a lot of stone for building and gold and silver. Like the Mayas, they (4) _____ (get) the liquid from rubber trees and (5) _____ (use) that, too. They (6) _____ (make) balls for their famous ball game and (7) _____ (use) it to clean their teeth after meals. They (8) _____ (invent) the first chewing gum! Rich Aztec people (9) _____ (wear) more clothes than poor people, and their clothes (10) _____ (are) made from different cloth. Poor people (11) _____ (can't) wear cotton. Women and girls (12) _____ (make) most of their clothes from the "century plant" and (13) _____ (use) bright colors and designs to decorate them. They (14) _____ (make) shoes from rubber, but if they (15) _____ (have) to go into a temple or see the king, they (16) _____ (can't) wear anything on their feet. When they (17) _____ (dance), they (18) _____ (wear) belts with seashells to make music as they (19) _____ (move). They sometimes (20) _____ (wear) feathers and animal fur, too. Aztec warriors (21) _____ (paint) their faces to look terrible and to make people afraid of them. Married women (22) _____ (put) their hair up on top of their heads. Corn (23) _____ (is) their most important food, but they also (24) _____ (eat) a lot of vegetables. They (25) _____ (don't eat) a lot of meat, but they sometimes (26) _____ (eat) insects and lizards.

Do you remember?

1 It might _____rain_____ later, so I'm going to take an umbrella.
2 I need to study because we _____ have a math test tomorrow, but I'm not sure.
3 I have a new _____ so my pants don't fall down.
4 When it's cold, I wear _____ on my hands.
5 People sewed _____ into their clothes 300 years ago.
6 _____ are usually made of nylon or wool.

Can do

I can talk about possibility using *may* and *might*.

I can talk about clothes.

I can write about my favorite clothes.

Remember to complete the online activities for this unit on Practice Extra.

What happens to our old sneakers?

1 **Read and write "could" or "if."**

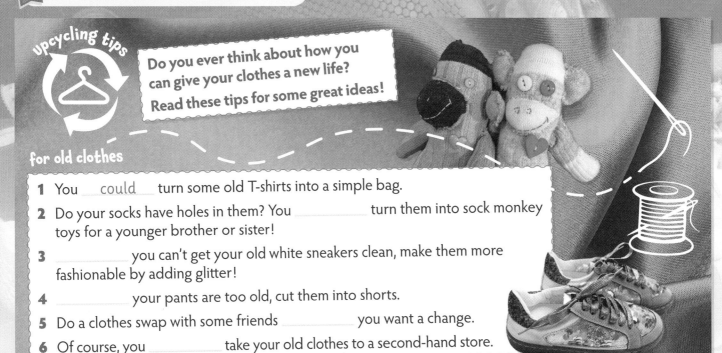

upcycling tips

Do you ever think about how you can give your clothes a new life? Read these tips for some great ideas!

for old clothes

1 You ___could___ turn some old T-shirts into a simple bag.

2 Do your socks have holes in them? You _____ turn them into sock monkey toys for a younger brother or sister!

3 _____ you can't get your old white sneakers clean, make them more fashionable by adding glitter!

4 _____ your pants are too old, cut them into shorts.

5 Do a clothes swap with some friends _____ you want a change.

6 Of course, you _____ take your old clothes to a second-hand store.

2 **Plan to write a brochure. Complete the table about how to upcycle clothes.**

Upcycling project:	
Information	Do you ever think about _____ ?
	Did you know that _____ ?
Advice	Here are some ideas to make your _____ last longer.
	You could _____ .
	You could _____ .
	If _____ .
	If _____ .

3 📝 **Use your notes to write your brochure.**

4 **Did you ...**

- ☐ plan your brochure?
- ☐ include some information and advice on your item of clothing?
- ☐ use *could* and *if* to give advice?
- ☐ check grammar, spelling, and punctuation?

Writing tip

Writing a brochure

A brochure gives information and advice to help other people decide what to do. When you give advice, use *could* and *if*.

If you don't like your old clothes anymore, you **could** give them to a friend.

Design: fashion and the environment | 🛡 social responsibilities

Flyers Listening

1 🎧 22 **Listen and check (✓) the box. There is one example.**

What has Holly put on to go to the park?

A ✓   B ☐   C ☐

1 Where has Richard left his umbrella?

  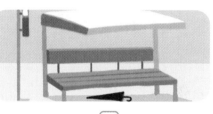

A ☐   B ☐   C ☐

2 Where is William going to go for his vacation?

  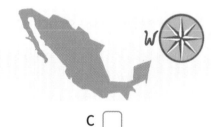

A ☐   B ☐   C ☐

3 Which pants will Emma wear to the party?

 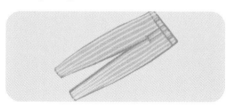 

A ☐   B ☐   C ☐

4 Where is Helen's brown belt now?

  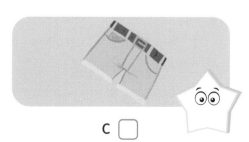

A ☐   B ☐   C ☐

8 Around the world

Have you finished **yet**?	I've **just** finished this book.
I haven't finished **yet**.	I've **already** finished my project.

 1 **Find two irregular past participles for each group of letters.**

1 b- _been_ , _begun_
2 m- ,
3 dr- ,
4 t- ,
5 th- ,
6 br- ,

7 sp- ,
8 l- ,
9 c- ,
10 st- ,
11 r- ,
12 go- ,

aught   ome   ood   ought   eant   ~~een~~   eft   ost   aken

rown   ent   oken   ne

un   olen   oken   aught   tten   ought   ~~egun~~   et   iven   idden   awn

 2 **Complete the sentences with verbs from Activity 1.**

1 He's r_idden_ his bike for two hours.
2 They've just g_____ out.
3 This is the third time I've b_____ to read this book!

4 She hasn't s_____ all her money yet.
5 Our cat still hasn't c_____ home.
6 They've just d_____ a picture.

3 **Look and write sentences with "already," "yet," or "just."**

1 (get up) She's just gotten up.
2 (clean her room) She hasn't cleaned her room yet.
3 (make her bed) _____
4 (put on her shoes) _____
5 (have breakfast) _____
6 (put on her pants) _____

4 **Write sentences about you today. Use "already," "yet," or "just."**

1 (have lunch) I've already had lunch. / I haven't had lunch yet. / I've just had lunch.
2 (read something) _____
3 (do some of my homework) _____
4 (listen to music) _____

Language: present perfect with *just, yet, already*   ▶ Do the online activities on **Practice Extra** as you complete this unit.

Mark (✓) two more correct sentences. Correct two more sentences.

1 "Clean your room!" "I've already cleaned it!" ✓
2 He is done his homework already. *He's already done his homework.*
3 Has he been to Australia?
4 I live here for ten years.
5 They's seen that movie already.
6 She's studied English for three years.

 What have they just done? Complete the sentences.

He's just cleaned his room _____ . She _____ . They _____ .

She _____ . We _____ . He _____ .

 Look at the Hirds' plans. Read and answer "Yes, they have." or "No, they haven't."

Vacation!

		morning	afternoon
Monday	Cambridge	see the university	play in a park
Tuesday	Nottingham	see the castle	ride bikes in Sherwood Forest
Wednesday	Liverpool	cross the River Mersey	go shopping
Thursday	York	have a picnic near the Roman walls	go to the Viking Museum
Friday	London	visit the Science Museum	take a picture of Big Ben

Now it is Wednesday lunchtime.

1 The Hirds haven't seen Cambridge University yet. *Yes, they have.*
2 They've already ridden bikes in Sherwood Forest.
3 They've already crossed the River Mersey.
4 They haven't had a picnic near the Roman walls .
5 They've already taken a picture of Big Ben.
6 They haven't visited the Science Museum yet.

Label the car stickers with nationalities. Use the letters in the box.

(**E**)   (**GR**)

(**IND**)   (**D**)

1 Spanish   3 _____

(**BR**)   (**P**)

(**F**)   (**MEX**)

2 _____   4 _____

5 _____   7 _____

6 _____   8 _____

Letters box:
```
a̶ a a a a a c c d
e e e e e e e g h̶
h i̶ i i i k l m n̶
n n n n n o p̶ r
r r r r s̶ s t u u x
z B F G G I M P s̶
```

 What countries are these web pages from?

www.mundocrianças.br   1 Brazil

www.xiaohaizi.cn   2 _____

www.niñolandia.es   3 _____

www.mondenfant.fr   4 _____

www.kidsofindia.in   5 _____

www.sunfun4kids.gr   6 _____

www.4crianças.pt   7 _____

www.mundoniños.mx   8 _____

 Read and answer.

Did you know that there are 195 countries in the world? Each of them has a capital city. Some of them even have more than one capital, and South Africa has three capitals! Some capitals aren't difficult to learn. For example, it's easy to remember that Mexico City is the capital of Mexico or that Brasilia is the capital of Brazil. We know the names of other capitals because we hear about them in classes at school, on the news, or during sports events.

You might know that the capital of Spain is Madrid and the capital of Greece is Athens. You may even know that the Chinese capital is Beijing or that the Portuguese capital is Lisbon, but did you know that the Indian capital is New Delhi? Some capitals surprise us because they aren't the biggest city in the country. Did you know that the capital of Australia isn't Sydney? No, it's Canberra. And the capital of the U.S.A. isn't New York; it's Washington D.C.

1 What's the Mexican capital? It's Mexico City.

2 What's the capital of India? _____

3 Which country is Canberra the capital of? _____

4 What's the name of the Chinese capital? _____

5 What's the Spanish capital? _____

6 What's the capital of Portugal? _____

7 Which country is Washington D.C. the capital of? _____

8 What's the Brazilian capital? _____

Complete the words with the groups of letters in the box. Use each group for only one pair of words.

al   any   ch   co   ey   ~~me~~   sh   tal   th   try

1	Ro…	*me*	…tal	Yes	(No)	6	Portug…	_____	…ready	Yes No
2	Turk…	_____	…es	Yes	No	7	capi…	_____	…lest	Yes No
3	coun…	_____	…ing	Yes	No	8	Engli…	_____	…orts	Yes No
4	Germ…	_____	…where	Yes	No	9	nor…	_____	…rown	Yes No
5	Fren…	_____	…opsticks	Yes	No	10	Mexi…	_____	…mb	Yes No

 Say the pairs of words in Activity 1. Do the letters sound the same in both words? Circle "Yes" or "No."

Rome … metal

 Ask and answer. Write your partner's answers.

1 Have you ever eaten Spanish food? _____ What was it? _____
2 Have you ever eaten Mexican food? _____ What was it? _____
3 Have you ever eaten Indian food? _____ What was it? _____
4 Have you ever eaten Portuguese food? _____ What was it? _____
5 Have you ever eaten Italian food? _____ What was it? _____
6 Have you ever eaten Chinese food? _____ What was it? _____
7 Have you ever eaten _____ food? _____ What was it? _____
8 Have you ever eaten _____ food? _____ What was it? _____

 Write a report about international food that you and your partner have eaten.

We haven't eaten Chinese food, but I've eaten Portuguese food. I can't remember the word, but it was fish with tomatoes. It was delicious. Igor's eaten Mexican food.

Sounds and life skills
Understanding responsibilities

Pronunciation focus

1 🎧 23 **Listen and underline the stressed words.**

1 I've <u>already</u> <u>cleaned</u> my <u>desk</u>.
2 Wait! I haven't saved the article yet!
3 Have they given the names of the competition winners yet?
4 We've just won new tablets for everyone in our class!

2 **Complete. Then practice saying the sentences.**

1 I've already _____ .
2 Wait! I haven't _____ yet!
3 Have they _____ yet?
4 We've just _____ !

3 **Read and match.**

1 bus driver   I've just seen an island.   I haven't sung in Rome or London.
2 chef   I've sung in New York and Paris.   I haven't explored it yet.
3 journalist   I've already designed the rocket.   I've just taken the children to school.
4 pirate   I've already made the salad.   I haven't written the story yet.
5 pop star   I've already taken pictures.   I haven't built it yet.
6 engineer   I've already washed the bus.   I haven't made the apple pie yet.

4 **Read and complete.**

Every day, I have to _____ .
Before I go to school, I have to _____ .
At school, I need to _____ and _____ .
After school, I have to _____ .

Sounds and life skills: stressed words | 🛡 critical thinking

8

1 Read and answer.

Diggory Bones

1 What's Iyam just done? He's just pushed the corn symbol.
2 How long has the museum at Balankanché been open? _____
3 How did the Mayas water their fields? _____
4 How long have Interpol wanted Iyam and Richard Tricker? _____
5 What are Sir Doug Bones and Diggory going to do with the Sun Stone? _____
6 What did Emily's grandfather use to follow them? _____

2 Do the quiz. Circle T (true) or F (false).

1 The Aztecs built the modern day Mexico City on a lake called Texcoco because they saw a Quetzal bird there. **T / (F)**
2 The Mayas studied the sun, the moon, and the stars to measure time. **T / F**
3 For the Aztecs, gold was the most important material in their lives. **T / F**
4 The Mayas used symbols or "glyphs" to communicate in writing. **T / F**
5 The Mayas played musical instruments made of turtle shells, wood, and seashells. **T / F**
6 The Pyramid of Kukulcán sounds like a Quetzal bird singing when someone climbs it. **T / F**
7 The Mayas played a ball game called Tlachtli. It's like volleyball and basketball. **T / F**
8 Aztec braves painted their faces and wore birds' feathers and animal fur to look beautiful and to make people love them. **T / F**
9 The first chewing gum was made from soft rubber from trees. The Mayas used it to clean their teeth. **T / F**
10 The form of a snake moves up and down the north stairs of the Pyramid of the Sun. **T / F**

Do you remember?

1 It's seven o'clock in the evening. Have you done your homework ___yet___ ?
2 Yes, I've _____ finished it! I finished it ten seconds ago.
3 Paris is the _____ of France.
4 People in Mexico speak _____ .
5 I have been to Germany and France, but I can't speak _____ or _____ .
6 Beijing is the capital of _____ .

Can do

I can talk about what has happened using *just*, *already*, and *yet*.

I can talk about different countries and nationalities.

I can write about things I've done.

Which countries do people visit the most?

1 **Read and match.**

My vacation in Malaysia

1 The capital city of Malaysia is Kuala Lumpur, which is also the
2 In Kuala Lumpur you can visit the tallest
3 Malaysian food is amazing, and the most
4 I think the most beautiful
5 There is a lot of traffic, so for me, the

a park is KLCC Park downtown.
b biggest city.
c easiest way to travel around the city is by train.
d twin skyscrapers in the world – the Petronas Twin Towers.
e popular dish is *nasi lemak*, which is rice cooked in coconut milk.

2 **Plan to write a blog post. Complete the table about a vacation.**

Paragraph 1 Where did you go? When did you go? Who did you go with?	I went to _____ on vacation. I went on/in _____ . I went with _____ . We stayed _____ .
Paragraph 2 Where is it? What else do you know? What is it famous for?	_____ is a town/city/country in _____ . The official language is _____ . The weather there is _____ . It is famous for its _____ .
Paragraph 3 What did you see/do/eat?	For me, the most interesting place was _____ . The best thing I saw was _____ .
Paragraph 4 How do you feel about your vacation?	It was _____ . _____ .

3 📝 **Use your notes to write your blog post.**

4 **Did you ...**
- ☐ plan your blog post?
- ☐ talk about what to see, do, and eat?
- ☐ use superlatives?
- ☐ read your blog post again?
- ☐ check your grammar, spelling, and punctuation?

Writing tip

Writing a blog post

We use **superlatives** to describe things. You can use superlatives in a blog post to give more information and describe how you felt.

The **best** thing to do there is ...
The **hottest** season is ...

Math: graphs and charts | learning to learn

Flyers Reading and Writing

1 **Read the diary and write the missing words. Write one word on each line.**

Example	This evening, I'm writing my diary ___in___ Paris!
1	Paris is the capital of _____. I'm here because I want to learn
2	to _____ French better and to see the city, of course. Today I
3	_____ to the Eiffel Tower with my friends. It's really tall, and
4	it looks very beautiful. I _____ some great pictures.
5	Tomorrow we're _____ to visit a famous museum called the
	Louvre, so we can see the *Mona Lisa*. I can't wait!

Review Units 7 and 8

1 **Read the story. Choose a word from the box. Write the correct word next to numbers 1–8.**

> belt   button   capital   clothes   different   ~~just~~   pants   Paris
> pockets   same   shorts   Spanish   T-shirt   umbrellas   worn

FRIENDLY

Sally, Eva, and Robert are sad because the second season of *Friendly* has _____just_____ ended. They all agree that the funniest episode of this season was "Jim's new clothes."

In the episode, Jim and Peter went to London to buy some new clothes. They caught the train to the (1) _____ one Saturday morning. They found a store called Fine Fashion. The salesman told them that all the clothes came from (2) _____, the capital of France and the capital of fashion.

Jim bought some big green pants with (3) _____ above the knees. He bought a light-gray T-shirt and a black (4) _____. He liked his new (5) _____, and he decided to wear them home.

When they went back to the station, they saw Jim's grandfather, but it was very funny because his grandpa's (6) _____ were big and green with pockets above the knees. He was also wearing a light-gray (7) _____ and a black belt. His clothes were the (8) _____ as Jim's!

2 **Choose a title for this episode of *Friendly*.**

Mark (✓) one box.   Streets ahead ☐   Capital cities ☐   The latest fashion ☐

3 **Read the jokes. Match the questions to the answers.**

1	What do you call an elephant at the North Pole?	a	Anything! It can't hear you!	☐
2	What did the scarf say to the hat?	b	A monkey!	☐
3	Why do birds fly south in winter?	c	A spoon!	☐
4	What do we have to break before we can use it?	d	Lost!	1
5	What kind of key opens a banana?	e	Because it's easier than walking!	☐
6	What do you get if you cross a kangaroo with an elephant?	f	Halfway. Then you're walking out of a forest.	
7	What do you call an elephant with a carrot in each ear?	g	You go on ahead, I'll just hang around.	☐
8	How far can you walk into a forest?	h	Big holes in Australia!	☐
9	What's the best thing to put into ice cream?	i	An egg!	☐

Complete the sentences. Count and write the letters.

1   Shorts   are short pants. We wear them in the summer. 6

2 Hindi, French, and Portuguese are different _____ . ☐

3 We wear _____ on our hands. ☐

4 A hundred years is a _____ . ☐

5 He's just _____ his coat on. He's going out. ☐

6 Africa is a _____ . ☐

7 You might have a _____ inside your jacket. You can carry things in it. ☐

8 The cities of London, Paris, and Rome are all _____ . ☐

9 We use this to close our shirts and coats. It can be different shapes and colors.

_____ ☐

10 We wear a _____ at the top of our pants or jeans so they don't fall down. ☐

11 What _____ is she?" "She's Chinese." ☐

12 Oh, no! It's just started to rain, and I've left my _____ at home! ☐

13 Special clothes to protect us. A firefighter wears one. ☐

5   **Now complete the crossword. Write the message.**

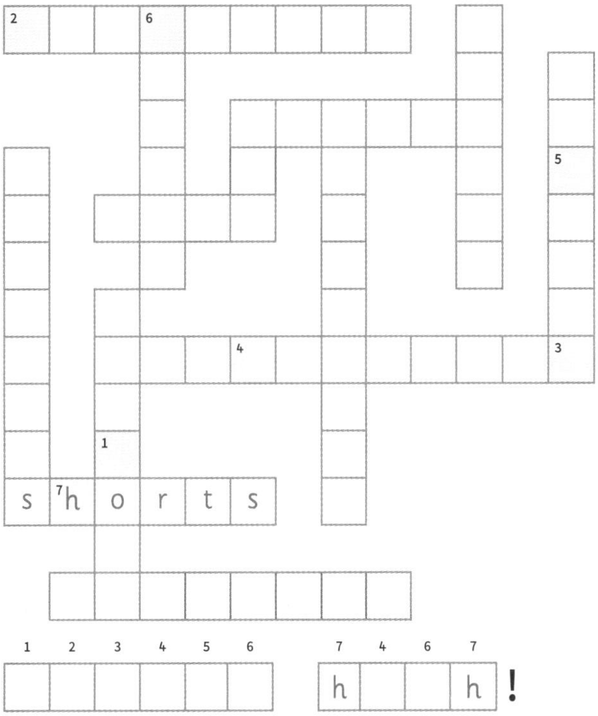

(crossword grid with clue numbers 1–7; filled answer reads: s ⁷h o r t s)

1 2 3 4 5 6   7 4 6 7
☐☐☐☐☐☐   h ☐ h !

6   **Quiz time!**

1 Why was Robert's shirt funny at the dance?
  It was _____

2 When did people start wearing sneakers?
_____

3 How long does plastic take to decompose?
_____

4 How many countries won the blog competition? _____

5 Where is sushi from? _____

6 What was the most popular country for people to visit in 2019? _____

7   **Write questions for your quiz in your notebook.**

Living with technology

1 Read and answer.

David's older sister, Jenny, thinks he has a problem with computers. He spends more than two hours a day in front of the screen, and he's very unhappy when he doesn't have an internet connection. He spends all weekend at home playing on the computer, and he doesn't want to go out with his friends.

When his parents call him for family meals, he takes about ten minutes to go to the table. Then he gets angry when he has to help the family clean up after the meal. He only wants to go back to the computer. Last Sunday, Jenny saw him playing video games at three o'clock in the morning when the family were all in bed.

1 Who thinks David has a problem? _Jenny thinks he has a problem._

2 How much time does he spend on the computer every day? _____

3 Why doesn't he want to go out with his friends? _____

4 What was he doing at three o'clock in the morning last Sunday? _____

5 Do you think David has a problem? _____

6 What do you think Jenny should do? _____

2 Write sentences with "should" or "shouldn't."

1 be careful / talk to / internet _You should be careful who you talk to on the internet._

2 spend time / in front of / screen _____

3 be afraid / use technology _____

4 play video games / at night _____

5 get angry / use technology _____

Values: units 1 & 2 *Living with technology* | social responsibilities

1 **Read and choose the answer.**

www.lottaquizzes

How safe are you?

1 Your little sister's hands are dirty from playing in the garden. There are some cookies on the kitchen table. What should you tell her to do?

a Clean her hands on her pants and take a cookie.

b Eat two cookies quickly before your parents come.

c Wash her hands and then have a cookie.

2 There's a heavy box of books on your bedroom floor. You have to take them to the car. What should you do?

a Put the books into two boxes and carry first one, then the other to the car.

b Pick up the box. It's difficult, but you try to take it very quickly.

c Ask your little sister to carry the box for you.

3 You want to get a glass from the highest shelf in the cupboard. What should you do?

a Climb onto a chair and lift your hands above your head to get it.

b Ask your mom or dad to help you.

c Pick up your little brother and put him on your shoulders so he can get it for you.

4 You've dropped a bowl of water on the kitchen floor. What should you do?

a Dry the floor carefully because it's dangerous to walk on.

b Go outside and play. Somebody else can clean it up.

c Put a chair over the water so nobody can see it.

2 **Write a safety contract for your home.**

1 We have to put our toys away safely.

2 _____

3 _____

4 _____

5 _____

_____ got the Safety at Home Certificate.

✓ **Congratulations!**

1 **Read and choose the right words.**

Mei Li's family lives in a big (1) **country /** (city) **/ continent** in China. She lives at home with her grandparents, her mom, her younger brother, and her younger (2) **brother / sister / aunt**. In her family, (3) **everyone / anyone / everywhere** helps at home. Her grandparents take care (4) **under / at / of** the children when their mom is working. Mei Li likes to help her family, so she takes her brother and sister to kindergarten (5) **before / after / since** she goes to school. After school, her brother (6) **feeds / waters / eats** the plants, her sister takes out the trash, and Mei Li (7) **washes / cooks / cleans** dinner. The (8) **children / animals / cousins** all clean their own bedrooms.

2 **Write about how you help at home. Use the pictures and questions to help you.**

- What jobs do you do at home?
- What jobs do your mom, dad, brothers, and sisters do?
- Do you enjoy doing jobs at home? Why? Why not?
- How do you feel when you help at home?

At home, I do several things to help.

Units 7&8 Values Sharing problems

1 Read and answer.

1 There's a new boy at school. How can you help him make friends?

2 Some children at school have started calling you terrible names. What should you do?

3 Your little brother has a big problem at school. He's asked you not to tell anybody. You think the problem is serious. What are you going to do?

4 Your group of friends at school doesn't like another student. They've told you not to spend time with this student or they won't talk to you. What should you do?

5 One of your friends has sent some mean messages to another student at school. What are you going to do?

2 Talk about your ideas with your partner. Do you agree?

I agree.

I don't agree. I think …

3 Read and match.

1	I'm very	a	I do?	☐
2	They think	b	angry.	1
3	This isn't	c	very worried.	☐
4	What should	d	help me.	☐
5	I'm	e	the first time.	☐
6	Please	f	it's funny.	☐

4 📝 In your notebook, write a message to a friend about a problem you have at school. Use the phrases from Activity 3 to help you.

5 Swap your message with a partner. Read the message and then give them some advice.

You should / shouldn't …

You have to …

The best idea is to …

It might be a good idea to …

Grammar reference

☆ **Complete the sentences.** [don't   Let's   should   Should   shouldn't   ~~Would~~]

1 _____Would_____ you like some ice cream?
2 You _____ play soccer in the street.
3 Why _____ we send her a text message?
4 _____ we chat online?
5 I _____ do my homework before I play on the computer.
6 _____ write an article for the blog.

1 Write questions. Answer.

1 he / be an actor? (✘)   Is he going to be an actor? _____ No, he isn't.
2 they / see a movie? (✓) _____
3 you / do your homework? (✓) _____
4 she / be in the play? (✘) _____
5 we / play tennis? (✘) _____
6 he / read a book about dragons? (✓) _____

2 Read and write.

1 They'll go to the moon by plane. (rocket) No, they won't. They'll go there by rocket.
2 She'll eat fruit. (special space food) _____
3 I'll wear jeans. (skirt) _____
4 They'll fly to Jupiter. (Mars) _____
5 We'll leave next week. (next month) _____
6 There'll be a lot of people. (robots) _____

3 Read and match.

1 I was snowboarding
2 They were waiting at the bus
3 She was making bread
4 We were having a picnic when
5 I was walking through the
6 He was sleeping when he

a felt a mouse in his sleeping bag.
b forest when I dropped my flashlight.
c when she lost her ring.
d when I fell and hurt my elbow.
e the storm began.
f stop when they saw their friend.

☐
☐
☐
[1]
☐
☐

4 Read and circle the correct word.

1 There are too (many) / any knives.
2 There **isn't** / **aren't** enough chairs.
3 She doesn't have **much** / **many** sugar.
4 They don't have **too** / **enough** forks.
5 Did they have **much** / **many** candy bars?
6 How **many** / **much** pasta do you want?

5 Complete the sentences. Write "for" or "since."

1 She's had her computer _____since_____ 2020.

2 We've studied English _____ five years.

3 I haven't played tennis _____ two weeks.

4 They've lived here _____ they were six.

5 He's been at his new school _____ three months.

6 She hasn't seen Peter _____ the summer.

6 Complete the sentences.

> any   anything   ~~Everything~~   no one   something   somewhere

1 It's raining.   Everything   in the backyard is wet.

2 I saw _____ interesting on TV last night.

3 The house was empty because _____ was at home.

4 He didn't have _____ money, so he didn't go to the movies.

5 I want to go _____ exciting for vacation this year.

6 Our town is really boring for young people. There isn't _____ to do.

7 Read and order the words.

1 [go to] [this evening.] [We might] [the movie theater]

We might go to the movie theater this evening.

2 [I'm tired.] [leave the dance] [I may] [early because]

_____

3 [They may not] [their project.] [have time] [to finish]

_____

4 [because of the snow.] [let us go home] [The teacher might] [early today]

_____

8 Write the sentences in the present perfect. Use the words given.

1 (just) I arrive at the airport. I've just arrived at the airport.

2 (yet) He not be to New York. _____

3 (already) I clean my room. _____

4 (yet) you write that email? _____

5 (just) He wake up. _____

6 (already) They finish the book. _____

Irregular verbs

Infinitive	Past tense	Past participle
be	was / were	been
be called	was / were called	been called
be going to	was / were going to	been going to
begin	began	begun
break	broke	broken
bring	brought	brought
buy	bought	bought
can	could	–
catch	caught	caught
choose	chose	chosen
come	came	come
cut	cut	cut
do	did	done
draw	drew	drawn
drink	drank	drunk
drive	drove	driven
eat	ate	eaten
fall	fell	fallen
fall over	fell over	fallen over
feel	felt	felt
find	found	found
find out	found out	found out
fly	flew	flown
forget	forgot	forgotten
get	got	gotten
get (un)dressed	got (un)dressed	gotten (un)dressed
get (up / on / off)	got (up / on / off)	gotten (up / on / off)
get to	got to	gotten to
give	gave	given
go	went	gone / been
go out	went out	gone / been out
go shopping	went shopping	gone / been shopping
grow	grew	grown
have	had	had
hear	heard	heard
hide	hid	hidden
hit	hit	hit
hold	held	held
hurt	hurt	hurt
keep	kept	kept

Infinitive	Past tense	Past participle
know	knew	known
leave	left	left
let	let	let
lie down	lay down	lain down
lose	lost	lost
make	made	made
make sure	made sure	made sure
mean	meant	meant
meet	met	met
put	put	put
put on	put on	put on
read	read	read
ride	rode	ridden
run	ran	run
say	said	said
see	saw	seen
sell	sold	sold
send	sent	sent
should	–	–
sing	sang	sung
sit	sat	sat
sleep	slept	slept
speak	spoke	spoken
spend	spent	spent
stand	stood	stood
steal	stole	stolen
swim	swam	swum
swing	swung	swung
take	took	taken
take a picture	took a picture	taken a picture
take off	took off	taken off
teach	taught	taught
tell	told	told
think	thought	thought
throw	threw	thrown
understand	understood	understood
wake up	woke up	woken up
wear	wore	worn
win	won	won
write	wrote	written